Studies in Discourse and Grammar

Studies in Discourse and Grammar is a monograph series providing a forum for research on grammar as it emerges from and is accounted for by discourse contexts. The assumption underlying the series is that corpora reflecting language as it is actually used are necessary, not only for the verification of grammatical analyses, but also for understanding how the regularities we think of as grammar emerge from communicative needs.

Research in discourse and grammar draws upon both spoken and written corpora, and it is typically, though not necessarily, quantitative. Monographs in the series propose explanations for grammatical regularities in terms of recurrent discourse patterns, which reflect communicative needs, both informational and socio-cultural.

Editors

Sandra A. Thompson
University of California at Santa Barbara
Department of Linguistics
Santa Barbara, CA 93106
USA

Paul J. Hopper
Carnegie Mellon University
Department of English
Pittsburgh, PA 15213
USA

Volume 16

Beyond Rhetorical Questions: Assertive questions in everyday interaction
by Irene Koshik

Beyond Rhetorical Questions

Assertive questions in everyday interaction

Irene Koshik
University of Illinois at Urbana-Champaign

John Benjamins Publishing Company
Amsterdam / Philadelphia

™ The paper used in this publication meets the minimum requirements of American National Standard for Information Sciences – Permanence of Paper for Printed Library Materials, ANSI Z39.48-1984.

Library of Congress Cataloging-in-Publication Data

Irene Koshik.
    Beyond Rhetorical Questions : Assertive questions in everyday interaction / Irene Koshik.
       p. cm. (Studies in Discourse and Grammar, ISSN 0928–8929 ; v. 16)
    Includes bibliographical references and indexes.
       1. Conversation analysis. 2. Questioning. I. Title. II. Series.

P95.45.K67 2005
401'.41--dc22   2005040616
ISBN 90 272 2626 1 (Eur.) / 1 58811 632 8 (US) (Hb; alk. paper)

© 2005 – John Benjamins B.V.
No part of this book may be reproduced in any form, by print, photoprint, microfilm, or any other means, without written permission from the publisher.

John Benjamins Publishing Co. · P.O. Box 36224 · 1020 ME Amsterdam · The Netherlands
John Benjamins North America · P.O. Box 27519 · Philadelphia PA 19118-0519 · USA

Table of contents

Acknowledgements · IX

CHAPTER 1
Introduction · 1
1.1 Interrogatives and "asking questions" · 1
1.2 Conversation Analysis methodology · 3
1.3 Organization of contents · 5

CHAPTER 2
Yes/no reversed polarity questions · 9
2.1 Introduction · 9
    2.1.1 Preference structure · 9
    2.1.2 "Conducive" yes/no questions · 10
    2.1.3 Questions as an expression of the speaker's epistemic stance · 12
    2.1.4 Relationship between questioner's epistemic stance and conduciveness or preference · 13
    2.1.5 Relationship between epistemic stance of question and epistemic authority of questioner · 13
2.2 Negative yes/no RPQs used as accusations · 17
2.3 Affirmative yes/no RPQs used to challenge recipients · 18
2.4 Challenges to non-present parties · 24
2.5 Repair initiations used as pre-disagreements · 27
2.6 Summary and discussion · 36

CHAPTER 3
Wh- reversed polarity questions · 39
3.1 Introduction · 39
3.2 Wh-questions used to challenge co-present parties · 41
3.3 Wh-questions used to challenge non-present parties · 49
3.4 Wh-questions used as complaints · 51

3.4.1 *How come* 51
3.4.2 *Why* 52
3.5 Wh-question challenges in institutional talk 54
3.6 Misunderstanding the sequential implicativeness of wh-questions 61
3.7 Summary of analysis 64
3.8 Canonical wh-question challenges 64
    3.8.1 *What do you mean* (+ X) 64
    3.8.2 *Who cares* 67
3.9 Interpretation of wh-question RPQs 69

CHAPTER 4
Yes/no reversed polarity questions used in pedagogically specific practices   71
4.1 Introduction 71
4.2 RPQs used as criticisms of student text 72
    4.2.1 Introduction 72
    4.2.2 RPQ with aligning response 73
    4.2.3 RPQ with non-aligning response 78
    4.2.4 RPQ sequence series 82
    4.2.5 Sequence and question design 92
    4.2.6 How these RPQs are interpreted as RPQs 96
4.3 RPQs used as hints in grammar correction sequences 99
    4.3.1 Introduction 99
    4.3.2 Preference structure of RPQs as hints 99
    4.3.3 Analysis of RPQ hints 101

CHAPTER 5
Alternative question error correction sequences   111
5.1 Other-initiated (OI) repair 112
5.2 Actions performed by OI repairs that repeat the trouble source 112
    5.2.1 Presenting candidate hearings for confirmation 113
    5.2.2 Displaying lack of understanding and eliciting an explanation 114
    5.2.3 Prompting for self-correction: Pre-disagreement 115
5.3 Actions performed by alternative question repairs 116
    5.3.1 Clarifying alternate hearings 117
    5.3.2 Clarifying alternate understandings 121
    5.3.3 Targeting errors and presenting candidate corrections 124

        5.3.4 Alternative question error corrections as vehicles
              for other actions   127
  5.4 Alternative question error corrections in pedagogy   129
        5.4.1 Error correction initiated on student talk   129
        5.4.2 Error correction initiated on student writing   131
        5.4.3 Evidence for canonical order of alternatives   132
        5.4.4 Providing candidate corrections after student failure
              to self-correct   134
        5.4.5 Disambiguating the first alternative   135
        5.4.6 Variations on alternative question error corrections   137
  5.5 Recognizing the actions performed by alternative
      question repairs   142
  5.6 Summary and discussion   144

CHAPTER 6
Conclusion   147
  6.1 Summary of findings   147
  6.2 Using questions rather than statements   150
        6.2.1 Challenges by broadcast news interviewers   150
        6.2.2 RPQ challenges in conversation   151
        6.2.3 Repetitions of a prior utterance, used as
              pre-disagreements and error correction
              initiations in mundane conversation   152
        6.2.4 Pedagogical interactions   153
  6.3 Final note   158

APPENDIX
Transcription symbols   161

Notes   163

References   169

Name index   175

Subject index   177

Acknowledgements

This book is truly collaborative in nature. It could not have been written without the training, support, feedback, and practical help of numerous others. I am grateful to Manny Schegloff for first inspiring me with his ability to see the details of social interaction, for his patient training in Conversation Analysis methodology, and for his continued mentoring and support. I am grateful to Steve Clayman and John Heritage for introducing me to the analysis of institutional talk, and for their training and their ongoing support and encouragement. Manny, Steve, and John have been models for me in mentoring my own students. I also want to thank the numerous colleagues from various data sessions and Conversation Analysis institutes for the opportunity to learn from them.

I am very grateful to those who have given me feedback over the years on various portions of this analysis, and to those who have read and commented on the entire manuscript. These include, among others, Marianne Celce-Murcia, Steve Clayman, Andrea Golato, Makoto Hayashi, John Heritage, Gene Lerner, Doug Maynard, Emanuel Schegloff, and Sandy Thompson.

I am also grateful to many colleagues here at the University of Illinois, Urbana-Champaign, both in my department and in cross-disciplinary groups, for their encouragement and support. In particular, I would like to thank Numa Markee, the Director of my department, for being supportive of my work and for providing me with a teaching sabbatical for one semester to work on the research for this book. I thank the Campus Research Board at the University of Illinois, Urbana-Champaign, for funding for additional data collection and research assistants to help transcribe data used for this book. My thanks also goes to my three research assistants for their invaluable help: Mi-Suk Seo and Minjung Park, for copying, transcribing and cataloging data, and Benjamin Willey, who assisted me for an extra semester with an enormous amount of work, including research; copying, transcribing, and cataloging data; and computer support. Finally, I would like to thank Sue Mauck for her help with the proofreading.

Portions of Chapter 2 and 4 have been published in *Journal of Pragmatics*, Vol. 34, No. 12 (Elsevier 2002). Portions of Chapter 3 have been published in *Discourse Studies*, Vol. 5, No. 1 (Sage 2002). Portions of Chapter 5 have been published in *Discourse Studies*, Vol. 7, No. 2 (Sage 2005). I thank the publishers for permission to reprint portions of the earlier articles in this manuscript.

I would like to thank all of those who so freely shared conversation analytic data with me, especially Manny Schegloff and John Heritage. I also thank Jo Hilder and Christine Holten who were invaluable in enabling me to collect the data and information I needed to begin my first analysis of the phenomena in this book. Jo shared many of her videotapes of teacher-student conferences and copies of student papers with me, and Christine shared her time and her expertise on teaching writing. Finally, I would especially like to thank all of the anonymous participants who allowed their interactions to be recorded. Without their generous willingness to participate, none of this research would have been possible. This book is dedicated to them.

CHAPTER 1

Introduction

This book uses conversation analysis methodology to analyze rhetorical and other questions that are designed to convey assertions, rather than seek new information. It shows how these question sequences unfold interactionally in naturally-occurring talk, what kinds of answers, if any, they engender, and how these answers display the recipients' understanding of the social actions that these questions are used to perform.

1.1 Interrogatives and "asking questions"

There is not a clear correspondence between questions, as a syntactic form, and asking questions, as an activity (Heritage & Roth 1995; Schegloff 1984). Quirk et al. (1985) and Weber (1993), list *declarative questions* as a category of question. These are declaratives, not syntactic questions, with rising intonation. However, declaratives with falling intonation can also be heard as asking questions, especially when they are "B-event" statements (Heritage 1985; Heritage & Roth 1995; Labov & Fanshel 1977), i.e., statements about a matter that the recipient has primary access to, or primary rights to know. These statements are treated as questions in that they make relevant a confirmation or disconfirmation. Heritage and Roth (1995:11) give the following example, asked by an interviewer during a broadcast news interview: "So in a very brief word David Owen you in no way regret what you did er despite what has (happened) in Brighton this week in the Labour Party."[1] The interviewee answers: "n- In no way do I regret it."

Similarly, syntactic questions are not always used to ask questions, in the sense of seeking new information (Schegloff 1984). Questions are commonly used as a vehicle for doing other actions, for example invitations: "Why don't you come and see me sometimes." (Schegloff 1984), offers: "Would you like a cup of coffee?" (Schegloff 1995b, to appear), complaints: "Why is it that we have to go there." (Schegloff 1984), and requests: "Kin I hev yer light?" and (at the beginning of a phone conversation) "Is Judy there?"(Schegloff 1995b, to appear).

One type of syntactic question that is regularly understood to be doing something other than asking questions is the rhetorical question. Many people think of rhetorical questions as questions that are not meant to be answered, possibly because the answers are obvious. But when we look at how these questions are actually used in interaction, they do sometimes get answers. Something these questions all have in common, however, is that they are not asked, and are not understood, as ordinary information-seeking questions but as making some kind of claim, or assertion, an assertion of the opposite polarity to that of the question. Quirk et al. (1985:825) explain that "a positive rhetorical *yes-no* question is like a strong negative assertion, while a negative question is like a strong positive one." They give the following (constructed) examples (826):

(1) POSITIVE:
Is that a reason for despair? ['Surely that is not a reason ...']
NEGATIVE:
Isn't the answer obvious? ['Surely the answer is obvious.']

Similarly, Freed (1994) writes of questions that do not seek information, but convey information to the hearer.

Their ability to convey assertions opposite in polarity to that of the question allows these questions to be used in specific ways to accomplish specific kinds of social actions. Because the term *rhetorical question* is potentially misleading, I will use the term *reversed polarity question*, or *RPQ*, to refer to these questions from now on. The term *RPQ* will also allow me to capture the relationships among a wider variety of practices, some of which are not thought of as *rhetorical questions*.

RPQs, as they are used in naturally-occurring talk, have not been studied extensively from either a linguistic or a language and social interaction perspective. Linguists such as Bolinger (1957) and Quirk et al. (1985) include brief descriptions of rhetorical questions among their categories of question types. But because their data are based on intuitions of how these questions are used, this literature does not allow us to see to what extent these questions are actually used in naturally-occurring talk, nor does it provide us with information on the interactional contexts of the talk in which these questions are used. This information is necessary to understand what social actions RPQs are being used to accomplish, and how they accomplish these actions. Within the framework of language and social interaction, reversed polarity questions have not yet been studied as a class as they are used in naturally-occurring talk. Only a small subset of negatively-formatted RPQs have been described, as they are used by broadcast news interviewers in hostile questioning (Clayman & Heritage 2002; Heritage 2002a, 2002b). There is also a work in progress that is currently investigating RPQs used in Korean complaint sequences (Yoon in progress).

This book investigates RPQs used in naturally-occurring interactions in many kinds of speech events: ordinary conversation, news interviews, teacher-student talk, and in different cultural settings, from American friends arguing over the phone, to international students in an English-speaking environment, to tribal people in small villages in Papua New Guinea. Across these widely-different contexts, the questions are used in some strikingly similar ways, as accusations, challenges to prior turns, complaints, pre-disagreements, or to target problems in a prior utterance. They are also used in North American pedagogical talk as hints to enable students to perform error correction successfully. Using Conversation Analysis methodology, we will look in detail at individual segments of interaction in which these questions are being used to see how they are heard as making assertions rather than seeking information, what specific social actions they are being used to accomplish, and how they accomplish these actions.

1.2 Conversation Analysis methodology

Because Conversation Analysis (CA) methodology does not rely on theoretically generated categories of analysis but derives the categories of analysis from the data itself, it has enabled CA researchers to discover insights about how people "do talk-in-interaction" that were previously unavailable to intuition. Here is a brief summary of the methodology.[2]

CA data are taken from audio- and video-taped interactions and from transcripts of the talk and relevant nonvocal behavior. A CA analysis is data driven: categories of analysis are not determined beforehand but are those that the participants themselves display an orientation to in their talk. The focus of a CA analysis is on particular practices of talk-in-interaction, including nonvocal behavior, and on the actions that the talk is accomplishing (Schegloff 1995a, 1995b, to appear), as these are displayed turn-by-turn. By "practices", CA researchers refer to how the interaction is done, i.e. the way that the talk and other behavior such as gestures are designed, both at the turn level, and at the sequence level. Sequences are courses of action implemented through the talk (Schegloff 1995b, to appear). According to conversation analysts, this focus on action, i.e. what is being done through the "talk-in-interaction", is the orientation that participants themselves have to talk.[3] CA researchers employ categories taken from the members' perspective (ten Have 1999). However, in contrast to ethnographic research methods, these categories are not obtained by interviewing the participants; participants are rarely consciously aware of their talk or nonvocal behavior in the detail in which these are studied by conversation analysts. Rather, CA researchers observe what the participants themselves orient to in their talk and interaction.

How is this orientation discovered? A basic issue for analysis is set up by a basic question for conversationalists, which is, about anything that happens in the interaction, "Why that now?" (Schegloff & Sacks 1973). In other words, participants in conversation try to understand what co-participants are doing by saying a particular utterance at a particular point in the sequence of talk. Participants, in the course of interaction, regularly demonstrate their understanding of what other participants' talk is doing. They demonstrate this understanding to other participants as a natural process of responding to their talk, and this same demonstration of understanding is also available to the researcher. Analysts can use this displayed understanding to try to understand what sort of "that" triggers that issue for the participants, what sort of "now" it is embedded in, and what sort of accounts the participants come up with for it. CA analysts use information such as the location of the utterance in a larger sequence, and the property of *conditional relevance* (Schegloff 1968), which enables us to see utterances as connected: given a first item, i.e., an initiating action such as a question, or an invitation, the second is expectable, e.g. an answer, or an acceptance; if it does not occur it can be seen as officially absent (Schegloff 1968: 1083). A claim about what a particular utterance is doing requires evidence that the participants themselves have viewed the utterance in this way. CA transcripts are very detailed because it is not possible for an analyst to know beforehand exactly what aspects of the talk – or the silence – will turn out to be displayed as relevant.

The most common form which a CA analysis takes is a description of "the structure of a coherent, naturally bounded phenomenon or domain of phenomena in interaction, how it is organized, and the practices by which it is produced" (Schegloff 1987a: 101). To do this, CA researchers work with a collection of fragments of talk that exemplify the phenomenon or domain of phenomena being studied. Excerpts discussed in this book are thus taken from collections of similar practices, all of which show the participants' understanding of the practice, as this understanding is displayed during the course of their talk. A microanalysis such as this can show us in detail how a particular practice of talk comes to accomplish a particular social action, how it comes to be understood by the participants as doing that social action, and what its consequences are for subsequent talk. When a number of separate micro-analyses are done on related phenomena, they can form together a detailed picture that contributes to our understanding of macro issues in language and social interaction.

1.3 Organization of contents

The remainder of this book is organized as follows. Chapters 2–5 investigate different types of RPQs and the social actions they are used to accomplish. After establishing the relationship between the epistemic position from which yes/no RPQs are asked, the questioner's epistemic stance expressed through the question, and the "preference" for a particular answer, Chapter 2 discusses specific examples of yes/no RPQs used as challenges, either challenges of the recipient's actions in the exogenous context, or challenges of prior turns. The prior turns which RPQs challenge can consist of talk by co-present parties or the reported speech of non-present third parties. Examples from broadcast news interviewers involve grammatically negative questions, using the negative particle "not," e.g., "Didn't you ......" Interviewees regularly hear these questions as accusations, i.e., "You did ..." rather than as information-seeking questions, and respond with disagreements rather than answers (Heritage 2002a, 2002b). Grammatically affirmative yes/no questions can also be heard as reversed polarity assertions, i.e., in this case, as negative assertions. They are regularly used in a wide variety of contexts, from family arguments to news interviews, both as challenges to the recipient's actions or as challenges to prior turns of talk. An understanding of how affirmative yes/no RPQs are used to challenge prior utterances can help us to understand how some next turn repair initiations can be heard as pre-disagreements, and how they can be used to initiate error correction in pedagogical situations.

Chapter 3 begins with a discussion of challenges using wh-question RPQs, e.g. "when have I." said in response to an accusation that the questioner was in the habit of "blowing off girlfriends for guys". These RPQs are used to challenge a prior utterance, specifically to challenge the basis for or right to do an action done by the prior utterance. Like the yes/no RPQ challenges, these questions refer anaphorically back to the claim they are challenging, using adjacency, substitution, or incorporating elements of the prior claim into their design. Wh-

RPQs can also be used as complaints, challenging the appropriateness of an action. These questions target actions that may or may not be referred to in prior talk. As with the yes/no RPQs, wh- RPQs can be used to do challenging because they are understood as RPQs, as negative assertions. The wh-questions, however, perform these actions in a slightly different way. They are designed as requests for an account for a prior claim or action, but the implied negative assertion conveys that there is no adequate account available, and thus, that there are no grounds for the prior claim or action.

In Chapters 2 and 3, we see how RPQs can be used as challenges, pre-disagreements, or error correction initiations in a variety of settings. Those used in institutional settings can orient to institutional roles and norms and can help accomplish institutional goals, even though their design and the actions they accomplish are similar, both in and outside of the specific institutional settings. In Chapters 4 and 5 we see how the RPQ turns themselves, and/or the sequences of action in which the RPQs are used, can be designed to accomplish certain pedagogically-specific actions that are not generally done in ordinary conversation. The RPQ sequences discussed in these chapters are therefore practices of pedagogical talk, rather than ordinary conversational practices that happen to be used in a pedagogical setting.[4]

The RPQs analyzed in Chapter 4 are grammatically affirmative yes/no questions used by teachers in one-on-one post-secondary writing conferences on drafts of student essays. The writing conferences are held as part of a writing course for international and immigrant students enrolled at a large research university. Teachers use these yes/no RPQs as one of their resources to socialize students into the norms and practices of American written discourse. The questions are used to help students diagnose problems in two different types of sequences and in different sequential environments in the two sequences. These two different environments create different preferences for a response.

The first environment involves the use of RPQs in sequences focusing on enabling students to find problems with content and organization in their drafts, thereby ensuring that the students are able to solve these problems in a revision. For example, a teacher, after targeting a portion of student text as problematic, asks: "Is it relevant? to what you're saying?", implying, "It's not relevant to the thesis of your paper, and should therefore be left out." In these sequences, both teachers and students display an orientation to *no* or its equivalent as a "preferred" answer. The second environment involves the use of RPQs in sequences where teachers are assisting students to self-correct grammar errors. In these sequences, a course of action has already been implemented: eliciting a correct answer from the student. The RPQs are used as hints when the student displays problems finding the correct answer. The RPQs in this environment do not "prefer" *no* as an answer; in fact, the RPQs themselves do not receive an answer. The preferred response for an RPQ hint is the correct answer that it was used to elicit.

Chapter 5 discusses a pedagogically-specific type of alternative question used by teachers (or parents "doing teaching" with their children) to prompt learners to self-correct their errors, either oral or written. These questions present the learner with two alternative choices for an answer. The first alternative can function like the next turn repair initiators discussed in Chapter 2, i.e., a yes/no RPQ that repeats the learner's error, calling it into question. The second alternative provides a candidate correction. For example, a teacher, reading aloud from a student's text, "... potential affective," stops, and says "affective? or effective." The student replies, "effective." The first alternative can also function like the yes/no RPQs discussed in Chapter 4, targeting a portion of text and criticizing it. For example, after reading a student's summary of his paragraph, a teacher says: "allright. have you said that. (0.5) y- (0.5) in this.=or have you been really just talking about the common (1.5) common goal." Students regularly hear the second alternative as the "preferred" one.

The final chapter, Chapter 6, concludes with a summary of the findings and some observations on the use of questions, rather than statements, to perform the actions discussed in this analysis.

CHAPTER 2

Yes/no reversed polarity questions

2.1 Introduction

In this chapter we will first investigate yes/no RPQs used as challenges. These challenges are either challenges of the recipient's actions in the exogenous context, or challenges of prior turns of talk. The prior turns which RPQs challenge can consist of talk by co-present parties or the reported speech of non-present third parties. We will then investigate a related phenomenon: yes/no RPQs used as pre-disagreements. These RPQs target a prior turn of talk to elicit a backdown or an error correction.

Before I begin my analysis, I will introduce two concepts from two different bodies of literature that will be relevant to the analysis: *preference*, from the conversation analytic (CA) literature, and *conduciveness*, from the linguistics literature. I will then suggest an analysis, supported by data from both conversation and broadcast news interviews, for the relationship between the conduciveness of yes/no RPQs and preference structure. This analysis will form the basis for my subsequent analysis of yes/no RPQs in a number of different settings.

2.1.1 Preference structure

Both linguists and conversation analysts have addressed the issue of how certain yes/no questions can come to "prefer" one of the two alternatives, an affirmative or negative answer, over the other alternative. For conversation analysts, this is part of the organization of talk known as 'preference structure.' Many sequences, or "courses of action implemented through talk," (Schegloff 1995b: 3, to appear), are organized around the basic unit of the *adjacency pair*, consisting of two turns: a first pair part and a second pair part. Questions are first pair parts: they make relevant a certain type of response, an answer. Most first pair parts not only make relevant a certain type of response, they make relevant "alternative types of response" which "embody different alignments toward the project undertaken in the first pair part" (Schegloff 1995b: 58, to appear). Conversation analysts call these alternative types of response *preferred* and *dispreferred* responses (Pomerantz 1978, 1984; Sacks 1987 [1973]). The conversation analytic concept of preference does not refer to psychological preference, but to a structural relationship between parts of the sequence. Preferred responses are generally those that align with the activity that the first pair part seeks to accomplish.[5] For example, assessments generally prefer agreement, offers prefer acceptance, and requests prefer grantings. Dispreferred responses are generally those that do not align with this activity, e.g. disagreement, or rejection, or refusal. Preferred and dispreferred responses are often characterized by a contrasting set of features. Preferred responses are usually short, done without delay, and unmitigated. Dispreferred responses are often elaborated, delayed, and mitigated (Schegloff 1988b, 1995b, to appear).

Preference can not only be grounded in the trajectory of action begun by the first pair part. Preference can also be grounded in a different way: in the design of the turn which embodies the first pair part, e.g. through the grammar, prosody, or word selection (Schegloff 1995b, to appear). Schegloff (1995b: 62, to appear) discusses the following example of cross-cutting preferences, where the preference grounded in the course of action, and the preference grounded in the turn design, are opposite: "You're not going downtown, are you?" If this question is being used as a pre-request by someone wanting a ride, it would prefer a *yes* answer as a go-ahead for the request. However, grammatically, it is designed to prefer *no* as an answer. Yes/no questions seem especially likely to be designed grammatically to prefer answers which embody one of the two alternatives, *yes* or *no* (Heritage 2002a; Raymond 2000; Sacks 1987 [1973]; Schegloff 1995a, to appear).

2.1.2 "Conducive" yes/no questions

The concept of the *conduciveness* of yes/no questions parallels to some extent the concept of *preference* in the conversation analytic literature, especially, though not exclusively, preference grounded in the question design. According to Quirk et al. (1985: 808), conducive questions "indicate that the speaker is predisposed to the kind of answer he has wanted or expected." Quirk et al. give examples of grammatically negative questions which seem to expect negative answers, e.g. "Didn't he arrive yet?" and grammatically affirmative questions which seem to expect affirmative answers: e.g., "Did someone call?" They also give examples of questions that seem to reverse the polarity of their expected answer. According to Quirk et al., "Do you really want to leave now?", a grammatically affirmative question, expects a negative answer, and "Hasn't the boat left already?", a grammatically negative question, expects an affirmative answer. In these examples, the polarity reversal seems to be influenced by elements of the question design, the intensifier *really* in the former question, and the positive polarity item *already* in the latter question.

Bolinger (1957) relates conduciveness in yes/no questions both to elements of the question design and to what he calls the "assumption" of the speaker. Only negative questions, according to Bolinger, can be conducive. In order to distinguish between questions which he considers conducive and those he does not, Bolinger (1957: 102) puts the following invented example, "Isn't the sun shining?" in two different settings:

> A man's wife complains that she can't hang out the wash. In the first setting he is indoors and the blinds are drawn. He has no reason to assume that the sun is shining, and the [question] Isn't the sun shining? is a suggested explanation commutable with the [question] The sun isn't shining? ([similar to] Because the sun isn't shining?). In the second setting he is outdoors in full sunlight; his [question] is then conducive, and commutable with the [question] The sun is shining isn't it?

In the above example, only one of the two questions, the one said in full sunlight, is conducive according to Bolinger; it is a negative question that has an affirmative assumption. For Bolinger, conduciveness, and this reversal of polarity from negative to affirmative, is marked by the presence of an assumption, for example, something in the extra-linguistic situation such as "a remark about the sun shining in plain view of the facts," or linguistically, the presence of certain expressions which may mark an assumption (Bolinger 1957: 102). The question which seems to expect an answer of the same polarity as that of the question is the one asked "with the blinds down," i.e., the questioner does not know whether or not the sun is shining. The question which seems to prefer an answer of the opposite polarity is that asked "with the blinds up," i.e., the questioner has access to information which answers the question. The latter question acts then not as a "real" question, requesting information or even confirmation of a guess, but as an assertion, asked from a position where the questioner and the recipient of the question presumably have equal access to knowledge which answers the question. Quirk et al. (1985: 825), as we have seen earlier, describe similar types of questions under the category of *rhetorical questions*, which, they say, have "the force of a strong assertion."

As with Quirk et al.'s examples, Bolinger's example is a constructed example, as is the context in which it is put, so it cannot give us any information about the extent to which such utterances are actually said, if ever, or how they are used. His analysis also does not show us how the interpretation of a question's conduciveness is accomplished interactionally. I will turn now to examples of naturally-occurring talk which seem to support the intuitive analysis proposed by Bolinger and also show how the interpretation of the question's conduciveness is worked out interactionally.

2.1.3 Questions as an expression of the speaker's epistemic stance

If we look at examples from naturally-occurring talk, we see that certain questions do, indeed, appear to convey strong reversed polarity assertions, thereby displaying the epistemic stance of the speaker, i.e., that the speaker knows the answer to the question and knows it with certainty. There is evidence from broadcast news interviews that interviewees hear some yes/no questions, specifically grammatically negative questions beginning with phrases such as "Isn't it ..." or "Don't you ..." as affirmative assertions (Heritage 2002a, 2002b). The following example, (discussed in Heritage 2002a) is typical. The interviewer (IR) asks a grammatically negative yes/no question: it contains the contracted form of the negative *not*: "n't" (lines 1–7). The interviewee (IE), then President Clinton, reacts as if the interviewer were making the corresponding affirmative assertion:

```
(2)  Clinton Press Conference⁶
     01  IR:       W'l Mister President in your zea:l
     02             (.) for funds during the last
     03       -->  campaign .hh didn't you put the
     04             Vice President (.) an' Maggie and
     05             all the others in your (0.4)
     06             administration top side .hh in a
     07             very vulnerable position, hh
     08             (0.5)
     09  IE:       I disagree with that,=h (0.8) u-
     10             How are we vulnerable because .hh
     11             only vulnerable if you think it is
     12             inherently ba:d ta raise funds..hh
     13             and you believe that these
     14             transactions are between people
     15             who are .hh almost craven.=I mean
     16             (I do- wa-) that's how uh- I I (.)
     17             I don't agree with that. I .h
```

Clinton's response, "I disagree with that," (line 9), shows that he views the interviewer as having made an assertion that can be disagreed with. He goes on to specify the assertion that he has heard the interviewer making: that the members of the president's administration have been made vulnerable.

2.1.4 Relationship between questioner's epistemic stance and conduciveness or preference

The above example shows how certain interviewer questions can be treated by addressees and overhearers as making assertions of the opposite polarity to that of the form of the question. The capacity of these *reversed polarity questions (RPQs)* to act as assertions also suggests a way in which the questions can be heard as conducive, in the linguistic sense, or as preferring, in the CA sense, a certain answer, in this case, an answer of the polarity opposite to that of the question. Sacks (1987 [1973]:57), early in the history of conversation analysis, suggested that, "if a question is built in such a way as to exhibit a preference as between 'yes' or 'no,' or 'yes-' or 'no-' like responses, then the answerers will tend to pick that choice, or a choice of the sort will be preferred by answerers, or should be preferred by answerers." In other words, the answer is "'agreeing' with the preference" displayed in the question. I suggest that answers to RPQs agree with the implied assertion displayed in the question, and it is *in this way* that they agree with the preference of the question. These questions may therefore be designed, in the first instance, not to display an expectation for a certain answer, but to display the epistemic stance[7] of the speaker, sometimes acting more like assertions than questions. It is by virtue of this epistemic stance display that they may also prefer, in the CA sense, a specific answer, i.e., an answer that aligns with the stance displayed in the question. In other words, a *dispreferred* answer would be heard as a disagreement.

2.1.5 Relationship between epistemic stance of question and epistemic authority of questioner

It might be thought that the negatively-formatted design of the interviewers' questions discussed above plays a role in the questions' interpretation as reversed polarity assertions. However, not all similarly-designed negative questions from everyday conversation carry the force of reversed polarity assertions. This can be seen by comparing the news interview data with the following excerpt from ordinary conversation, discussed in Schegloff (1995b, to appear). In this example, the participants are local workmen who regularly meet and socialize in an upholstery shop owned by one of the group.

(3) **Upholstery Shop 24**
```
01  Mike:       Wanna get some- wannuh buy some
02              fish?
03  (Rich):     Ihh ts-t
04  Vic:        Fi:sh,
05  Mike:       You have a tank I like tuh tuh-
06              I-I [like-
07  Vic:           [Yeh I gotta fa:wty:: I
08              hadda fawtuy? a fifty, enna
09              twu[nny:: en two ten::s,
10  Mike:          [Wut- Wuddiyuh doing wit
11              [dem. Wuh-
12  Rich:  -->  [But those were uh:::
13              [Alex's tanks.
14  Vic:        [-enna five.
15  Vic:        Hah?
16  Rich:  -->  Those'r Alex's tanks weren't
17              they?
18  Vic:        Podn' me?
19  Rich:  -->  Weren't- didn' they belong tuh
20              Al[ex?
21  Vic:          [No: Alex ha(s) no tanks Alex
22              is tryintuh buy my tank.
```

As Mike begins introducing a proposal to buy a fish tank from Vic, and Vic enumerates the various sizes of tanks he has, Rich interrupts with an objection: "But those were uh::: Alex's tanks." (lines 12–13). It might be assumed that because the key element of Rich's assertion, "Alex's tanks", was said in overlap with the end of Vic's talk, Vic initiates repair with "Hah?" (line 15). A repair initiator can point to trouble hearing or understanding the target of the repair. It can also, however, point to trouble of another sort: a possible disagreement (Schegloff 1995b, 1997a, to appear; Schegloff et al. 1977), and indeed, Vic does end up expressing disagreement in lines 21–22.[8] In spite of the overlapping talk, which might suggest problems in hearing, Rich, in response to the repair initiator, does not simply repeat his previous utterance, which would indicate that he believed repair was initiated due to problems hearing his talk. He performs an action that is relevant after a pre-disagreement: a backdown (lines 16–17). And after a second repair initiator (line 18), he again performs a backdown (lines 19–20). The backdowns are achieved in each case by slightly weakening the epistemic strength of the assertion. At first Rich makes the assertion explicitly, with an affirmative statement: "But those were uh::: Alex's tanks." (lines 12–13). The second time, after the first repair initiator, he slightly weakens the epistemic strength; he makes the assertion explicitly in the first clause, and asks for confirmation in the tag: "Those'r Alex's tanks weren't they?" (lines 16–17). The final version, after the second repair initiator, weakens the epistemic strength even further, no longer making the assertion explicitly: "Weren't- didn' they belong tuh Alex?" (lines 19–20). This final question also does something more: it avoids a dispreferred response, in the face of a possible disagreement, by shifting the preference of the original utterance to one which is more likely to get an aligning response (Schegloff 1995b, to appear). "Weren't- didn' they belong tuh Alex?", in this context, seems to prefer the answer *no* as a response, which it does get (line 21) in a clearly preferred manner. This negatively-formatted question, similar in form to the news interview questions discussed above, does not display a strong affirmative assertion. On the contrary, it displays a weakening epistemic strength that suggests a preference for a same polarity answer.

Here is a similar example, also discussed in Schegloff (1995b, to appear), from a family dinner conversation. The older brother, Wes, is teasing his two younger sisters, 14-year-old Virginia and Beth, who is a college student. The "'er" in line 1 refers to Beth. Wes first makes an assertion and asks for confirmation of that assertion with a tag question. After repair is initiated on that question, he does a downgrade, demonstrating a weaker epistemic strength:

(4) **Virginia 14**
```
01 Wes:       =(Now) you taught 'er howda dance,
02            didn' y(ou)?
03            (1.0)
04 Vir:       Hu[h?      [Y:eah.
05 Wes:  -->     [Weren'[t you teachin' 'er some
06            new steps the othuh day?
```

That Wes's question in lines 5–6 is a downgrade, displaying doubt, is supported not only by the possibility that he can hear the one second silence (line 3) and Virginia's subsequent repair initiator "huh?" (line 4) as projecting a coming disagreement (though, as it turns out, there is no disagreement), but also by his weakening of the claim made, i.e., from teaching someone how to dance, to teaching someone "some new steps."

The interviewers' negative questions discussed in Heritage (2002a, 2002b) are heard by interviewees as strong affirmative assertions. Heritage (2002b) suggests that these questions are epistemically stronger than tag questions, as tag questions do not get responded to as assertions in news interviews. The above examples of negative questions from everyday conversation, however, seem to display a weaker epistemic strength than the corresponding tag question. Heritage's questions are clearly *reversed polarity questions*, said with a "blinds up" knowledge base: the questioner seems to be claiming access to information which answers the question. Broadcast news interviewers may be heard as implying that the assertions conveyed by their questions are common knowledge.[9] In Excerpt 3 above, the question, "Weren't- didn' they belong tuh Alex?", is being used to do a backdown in a sequence which demonstrates a successive weakening of the knowledge base of the questioner in the face of possible disagreement. Similarly, in Excerpt 4, the question, "Weren't you teachin' 'er some new steps the othuh day?" displays a weakening of Wes's claim in the face of a projected disagreement. In this case, the negative yes/no questions do not seem to be conveying the same type of reversed polarity assertion that the news interview questions claim. In fact, as already suggested, in the face of an incipient disagreement, they seem to prefer an aligning *no* answer of the same polarity as that of the question. In doing the questions as epistemic downgrades from the original assertions, the certainty of the knowledge base of the questioners is shown to be weakened, and this shifting epistemic environment produces questions that demonstrate doubt, i.e., "blinds down" situations, rather than conveying strong assertions of the opposite polarity.[10]

In the interpretation of yes/no questions as reversed polarity assertions, we can see that, as Schegloff (1997a) asserts, there is no one-to-one correspondence between form and action, in this case, between the design of the question and its interpretation as either a reversed polarity question or a "real" question, preferring an answer of the same polarity as that of the question. In Excerpt 3, the course of action implemented in the sequence, i.e., a series of repair initiations, and the successive weakening of Rich's epistemic certainty in response to these repair initiations, allow Rich's responses to be interpreted as backdowns. It is therefore both the course of action and the shifting knowledge state of the questioner which allow us to interpret the final question as one that displays doubt and seems to prefer an answer of the same polarity as that of the question, rather than as a reversed polarity assertion. A similar situation occurs in Excerpt 4. In contrast, the strong epistemic position from which the grammatically negative broadcast news interview questions are asked, claiming to evoke matters of public record, can contribute to their being heard as affirmative assertions. In the following analyses we will see how both a question's position in a particular course of action, and the displayed knowledge state of the questioner, helps determine whether the question is heard as an RPQ or as an ordinary, information-seeking question.

2.2 Negative yes/no RPQs used as accusations

We have seen how, according to Heritage (2002a, 2002b), interviewees respond to grammatically negative questions, asked from an interviewer's strong epistemic position, as affirmative assertions. We will now re-examine the Clinton interview discussed earlier to see how this polarity reversal enables the questioner to use these RPQs to make accusations against interviewees.

(5) **Clinton Press Conference**
```
01 IR:         W'l Mister President in your zea:l
02             (.) for funds during the last
03      -->    campaign .hh didn't you put the
04             Vice President (.) an' Maggie and
05             all the others in your (0.4)
06             administration top side .hh in a
07             very vulnerable position, hh
08             (0.5)
09 IE:  -->>   I disagree with that,=h (0.8) u-
10             How are we vulnerable because .hh
11             only vulnerable if you think it is
12             inherently ba:d ta raise funds..hh
13             and you believe that these
14             transactions are between people
15             who are .hh almost craven.=I mean
16             (I do- wa-) that's how uh- I I (.)
17             I don't agree with that. I .h
```

As discussed earlier, Clinton's response, "I disagree with that," (line 9), shows that he views the interviewer as having made an assertion that can be disagreed with. He goes on to specify the assertion that he has heard the interviewer making, i.e., that the members of the president's administration have been made vulnerable. We can see that he has heard this question as asserting an opinion rather than asking a question. The opinion Clinton has heard being asserted is hostile; the interviewer is accusing him of putting staff members in a vulnerable position. Clinton responds with a denial, challenging the interviewer's view of fundraising as exaggeratedly negative.

The next example, discussed in Heritage (2002a: 31), is similar. The interviewee treats the interviewer's question as if he were making corresponding assertions of the opposite polarity. He does this by expressing his disagreement, in particular, with the second of two assertions conveyed by the question. The interviewee is the US Ambassador to South Africa:

(6) US PBS Newshour: 22 July 1985
```
01 IR:  -->   But isn't this (.) d- declaration
02            of thuh state of emergency:: ( )
03            an admission that the eh South
04            African gover'ment's policies
05            have not worked, an' in fact that
06            the um- United States ( )
07            administration's policy of
08            constructive engagement ( ) has
09            not worked.
10 IE:  -->>  I do not agree with you .hhh that
11            the approach we have taken (.)
12            toward South Africa is- a- is an
13            incorrect approach.
```

As in the Clinton excerpt, the interviewer's question, in particular its second relative clause, is not only treated as an assertion but as an accusation against the interviewee. After expressing disagreement, showing his orientation to the interviewer's question as conveying an assertion (line 10), the Ambassador makes explicit the accusation he heard in the second part of the question, that the approach "we" have taken is incorrect (lines 10–13). The ambassador's "we" displays both his identity as a member of the administration and his understanding that he was among those being accused. Grammatically negative yes/no questions, when asked by interviewers, are thus regularly heard not only as affirmative assertions but as accusations.

2.3 Affirmative yes/no RPQs used to challenge recipients

The above examples all involve grammatically negative questions, using a contraction of the negative particle "not." As accusations, they could all be considered challenges to the recipient's actions. However, it is not only negatively-designed yes/no questions that are able to be heard as reversed polarity assertions. Grammatically affirmative yes/no questions are also regularly used in a wide variety of contexts, both as challenges to the recipient's actions or as challenges to prior turns. The prior turns which RPQs challenge can consist of talk by co-present parties or the reported speech of non-present third parties. In this section, we will look specifically at grammatically affirmative yes/no RPQs used to challenge the recipient's actions or prior talk.

The first example is taken from a PBS Newshour interview by Robert Mac-Neil of Lakhdar Brahimi, the UN Representative for Afghanistan, on October

27, 2001. They are discussing UN and US involvement in forming a new Afghan government.

(7) Newshour MacNeil/Brahimi10/27/01
```
01 LB:     so how fast we can:: (.) we can .h
02         we can get the afgha:ns to form a
03         government. (0.2).h I am not quite
04         sure at this stage.=
05 RM:     =.hhhhh secretary powell made it
06         (0.2) sound like a US operation
07         <with UN help.> (.) who is in
08         charge. (er)- are you? (.) is
09         the US:? (.) °who is it.°
10 LB:     I hope it's the afghans who are
11         going to be in charge,=an that
12         we are all helping them. .hh u:m
13         I was in washington: u:h (.) few
14         days ago: and we had uh (0.2) very
15         very fruitful discussions, .h
16         there is no:: no disagreement. .h
17         uh between us: and u:h the:
18         united states, .h u:h what united
19         states can do: (.) uh as (0.5) the
20         biggest power on earth, .h u:::h
21         is something, .h what the UN can
22         do is something else. (0.2) we
23         have we have different roles. .h
24         u:h (.) we desperately need the
25         united nations to b- the united
26         states to be engaged. .h and I
27         was: u:h (0.2) (I'm on I'm on)
28         record (0.2) .h fo:r criticizing
29         the united states for
30         [*not being engaged in the past.*
31         [(((*: smile voice))
32         .h so their engagement is is is
33         most welcome.
34 RM:     .h I [(guess)-
35 LB:          [I think that w- (0.2) u:h .h
36         >you know< we have a role to play,
37         =that is: the united nations on
38         behalf of the .h international
39         community,=and that includes
40         °of course the united states.°=
41 RM: --> =(e:) >I was wondering< can this
```

```
42        --> work. this (0.2) attempt to
43        --> encourage the afghans to
44        --> form: [a government.=can it work
45 LB:             [(uh huh)
46 RM:    --> .h if there is more than one cook
47        --> (.) stirring the broth.
48 RM:        .hh u:m h (0.5) u:h yes.=th- there
49            shouldn't be more than one cook to
50            stir the broth.=u:m,
51            (0.5)
52 RM:        and you are the cook?
53 LB:        u:h h .h (0.2) I am: whatever you
54            want me to be. u:h (0.5) what is
55            terribly important is that
```

After a question by MacNeil about who is in charge of the process of forming a new Afghan government, followed by two "candidate answers" (Pomerantz 1988) (lines 7–9), Brahimi begins discussing the roles of the various participants in this process, the UN, the US, and the Afghans themselves (lines 10–33, 35–40). MacNeil's follow-up question (lines 41–44, 46–47) is an RPQ conveying doubt that this joint operation proposed by Brahimi can work: "(e:) >I was wondering< can this work. this (0.2) attempt to encourage the afghans to form: a government.=can it work .h if there is more than one cook (.) stirring the broth." Embedded in the syntax of the question, is an account for why it can't work: "there is more than one cook (.) stirring the broth." (lines 46–47). Although it is designed as an "if" clause, this clause seems to be pointing out a problem with the joint operation proposed in Brahimi's prior turn, thus challenging his proposal. Brahimi responds to MacNeil's question as if it were an assertion (i.e., "It can't work if there is more than one cook stirring the broth"), His "yes" (line 48) is not an answer to MacNeil's yes/no question, "can it work …?" The continuation of Brahimi's turn, "there shouldn't be more than one cook to stir the broth" (lines 48–50), makes it clear that he is hearing the assertion conveyed by MacNeil's question and agreeing with it. But he avoids responding to the challenge to his own position implied in MacNeil's RPQ, i.e., that the joint operation cannot work *because* there is more than one cook stirring the broth.

Turning from broadcast news interviews to ordinary conversation, we see yes/no RPQs being used in similar ways to challenge utterances in prior turns. The following example is taken from an argument between a mother and her teenage son. The recording begins partway through the argument at a point where both the mother and son seem to be responding to accusations by the other party. The argument is quite heated, as evidenced by the capitalized letters showing louder than usual voices. The focal questions are two yes/no RPQs, one a syntactic statement, i.e., a "declarative question" (Quirk et al. 1985; Weber 1993) (line 22), the other a syntactic question (line 28).

(8) Marcia and Joseph

```
09 Mar:      I don't think I'm harming
10           anybu:ddy,
11           (0.3)
12 Jos:      AH WASN HARMING ANYBUDDY EITHER.
13           (0.5)
14 Mar:      Waddiyou mean you weren't harming
15           anyb[uddy
16 Jos:          [BY GOINGDA SCHOO:L WITH A
17           BROKEN COLLARBONE THAT GAVE YOU
18           THE PUNISHMENT 'N THE FIRS(T)
19           PLA[CE,
20 Mar:         [( )ING) ANYBU:DDY,
21           (0.9)
22 Jos: -->  I WAS HARMING YOU,
23           (1.2)
24 Mar:      ↑YE:AH:: YOU HAVEN'T LEARNED T'
25           GET ALO:NG HERE AT A:LL.=
26 Jos:      =I'M TALKING ABOUT GH*¹¹O:ING T'
27           SCHOOL with my broken collar
28      -->  bone.=Is that harming you,
29           (1.5)
30 Mar:      Why:- yes Joseph I happen t' be
31           the mother.
```

The RPQs are used by Joseph to challenge what appears to be an accusation by his mother. We don't have the original accusation on tape, but we do have a denial by Joseph (line 12) that he was harming anyone, and a challenge to this denial by Marcia (lines 14–15). We are thus already in a full-blown argument context by the time the first question is asked: "I WAS HARMING YOU," (line 22).[12] In this context, after Joseph's earlier claim (line 12) that he wasn't harming anybody, and Marcia's subsequent challenge to this claim (lines 14–15), "Waddiyou mean you weren't harming anybuddy" (Schegloff 1997a), his question is obviously not a request for information or for Marcia's opinion, but a further addition to the argument, conveying a stance that he wasn't harming Marcia. Joseph's stress on "YOU" may also contribute to this question being heard as a challenge. Marcia disagrees with this stance by giving an emphatic non-aligning answer to the question, "↑YE:AH::" (line 24), along with a further accusation, "YOU HAVEN'T LEARNED T'GET ALO:NG HERE AT A:LL." (lines 24–25). After a clarification, challenging Marcia's disagreement (lines 26–28), Joseph repeats his first question in a slightly different form: "Is that harming you," (line 28), and he gets another denial by Marcia, this time with an account (lines 30–31). The two questions are clearly RPQs used to convey an assertion of the opposite polarity, i.e., "I wasn't harming you", an opinion already expressed by Joseph in line 12 before either of the questions was asked.

Although the first RPQ in this excerpt is, like the others, an affirmative yes/no question that appears to be conveying a negative assertion, it differs in form from the RPQs discussed in Excerpts 5–7. It is done as a "declarative question," (Quirk et al. 1985; Weber 1993) and not as a syntactic question. However, like the RPQs discussed earlier, it is also used to challenge a recipient's prior utterance, to call it into question.

The final example is taken from a study of North American child language socialization by Taylor (1995), based on a videotaped family dinner conversation.[13] The family consists of Mom; Dad; Dick, 8 years 7 months; Janie, 5 years 11 months; Evan, 3 years 7 months; and Jon, 1 year 5 months. The RPQ (line 112) is asked by Dad to challenge an accusation by Janie that he and Mom were having a fight. There two segments of transcript separated by Taylor's summary of the intervening talk. The RPQ is in the second transcript segment.

(9) **Photo Negatives Story**

```
71 Dad:      Is it really ex-stremely
72           important to you to prove that
73           I did something wrong?
74           (0.6)
75 Dad:      [Is that- Is that ((to Mom,
76           [with emphatic gesture))
77 Mom:      [Not extremely important
78           [((half-laugh)) nho:?:
79 Dad:      ((nodding yes)) important enough
80           to carry it to this: - extre?:me
81           (0.8) ((Dad and Mom in
82           reciprocal gaze))
83 Dick:     ((standing behind chair,
84           whispering)) Daddy We're
85           [being filmed
86           [((Dad looks at Dick, shows no
87           reaction))
88 Mom:      nhh ((laughlike exhale?))
89           (4.0) ((Dad looks at plate, wipes
```

```
90             hands & mouth; Dick grins? at
91             Mom, then looks at floor; only
92             sound is parrot's chirping; Dad
93             begins to eat off Dick's plate;
94             Janie holds corn in front of
95             mouth, looks at Dad briefly; Mom
96             looks toward Dick and Janie))
```

At this point, Taylor (294) writes:

> The silence is finally broken by Janie, speaking for the first time since this story began: "Momma? (.) Is the film? (0.6) u:m (0.6) just picture or ((*nodding yes, facing Mom*)) talking too." Across several turns (deleted here), Mom and Dick clarify for Janie how the microphone works, until Mom sends Dick outside to check on the sleeping baby. Meanwhile, Dad remains suddenly silent, adding nothing in response to Janie's request for information. ... Janie ... after hearing these explanations and starting to eat again, nearly explodes with an epiphany-like realization that focuses on her parents' narrative-activity conduct and its consequences.

```
104 Janie:     (but-) (.) but ((turning to
105                      Mom)) .h (then it's) gonna hear
106                      your ((shouted whisper)) FI:GHT
107                      (0.8) ((Janie continues looking
108                      at Mom, next to her; Mom looks
109                      toward table or Dad?, who is
110                      eating continuously))
111 Dad:       ((eating, facing plate))
112       -->  You think it was a fight?
113            (0.2)
114 Janie:     ((with emphatic nod as she turns
115                      to Dad)) No
116 Mom:       hh hh hh hh .H ((slight bemused
117                      laugh, grinning))
118            (2.4) ((Dad keeps eating;
119                      Janie resumes eating))
```

Janie has obviously taken Dad's question, "You think it was a fight?" (line 112), as an RPQ criticizing her characterization of Dad's and Mom's prior talk as a "fight." Dad's contrastive stress on "fight" may contribute to this understanding. Even though Janie has just characterized this talk as a fight (lines 105–106) and has demonstrated sufficient concern about the seriousness of the fight to express her concern to Mom, on hearing Dad's question, she denies that she thinks it was a fight (line 115), agreeing verbally with the assertion conveyed through Dad's RPQ that there was no basis for her to consider this a fight, while at the same time nodding "yes". The verbal switch in stance is so abrupt, and the response so mixed, that Mom reacts to it with amusement (lines 116–117).

In the above excerpt, Janie reacts as if she has been sanctioned for characterizing her parents' talk as a fight. Schieffelin (1990), in a study of language socialization practices among the Kaluli of Papua New Guinea, also describes questions which are used to sanction children's behavior. She calls these questions "confrontational rhetorical questions" (87). They are used in Kaluli society to shame children into proper behavior. For example, a child who has taken someone else's property may be asked "Is it yours to take?!" (85). It is clear from the context in which these questions are used that they are also RPQs. The shaming quality may come from the fact that the questions refer to violated norms and the answer should be obvious to all present, including the sanctioned child.

Although several of the yes/no RPQs discussed above are done with contrastive stress, others have nothing in their design that could contribute to their being heard as RPQs. Each of these RPQs, however, is asked from the position of epistemic strength. Either the speakers have institutionally-oriented to claims to knowledge about the questions they are asking, as do broadcast news interviewers, or the question is asking about something already displayed to be in the speaker's knowledge domain. In Excerpt 8 Joseph has already given his opinion about whether he was harming anyone by going to school with a broken collarbone. In Excerpt 9, Dad can claim to have his own opinion about whether or not he was having a fight with Mom. His authority as a parent also could come into play in Janie's hearing of his question as an RPQ. Aside from epistemic strength, the sequential position of the questions can also contribute to their being heard as RPQs. They are more likely to be heard as challenges, rather than as questions, when challenges would be expected responses, e.g., after accusations. I discuss the importance of sequential position in more detail in the following chapter on wh-question challenges.

2.4 Challenges to non-present parties

Affirmative yes/no RPQs can also be used to challenge the talk of non-present parties. This talk is brought into the current sequence of talk as reported speech, and then subsequently challenged with an RPQ. RPQ challenges to talk of non-present parties can be used affiliatively or disaffiliatively, i.e., they can be used to align with or to challenge co-present parties. I will illustrate each type of alignment with broadcast news interview data. The first excerpt is taken from the same MacNeil/Brahimi interview from which Excerpt 7 above was taken. Robert MacNeil is interviewing the UN representative for Afghanistan, October 2001. The king referred to by MacNeil in this excerpt is the former Afghan king.

(10)   **Newshour MacNeil/Brahimi10/27/01:8:52-9:23**

```
01  RM:       .hhhh I believe you're going to
02            see the king.=in rome.=apart from
03            u:h uh uh in addition to other
04            p[eople.
05  LB:        [ultimately. yes.
06  RM:       ul[timately. u:h eh secretary
07  LB:        [(      mm hmm)
08  RM:       powell suggested the king would be
09            able to rally. (0.5) the different
10       --> elements. will he really,=because
11       --> some people are already calling
12       --> him irrelevant, or an a[merican
13  LB:                              [( )
14  RM: -->  puppe[t, or (.)
15  LB:          [°yeah.°
16            °yeah.° .h u:h you see we must be
17            [( )
18  RM:       [how important [is he.
19  LB:                      [(° °) I- I think
20            he is: he is imp- you know he
21            enjoy:s .h u::h respect in: many
22            quarters,
```

After getting confirmation that Brahimi will be seeing the former Afghan king in Rome (lines 1–5), MacNeil introduces reported speech by Secretary Powell with a footing shift (Clayman 1992): "u:h eh secretary powell suggested the king would be able to rally. (0.5) the different elements." (lines 6, 8–10). He then challenges that talk with an RPQ: "will he really,=because some people are already calling him irrelevant, or an american puppet, or (.)" (lines 10–12, 14). As Brahimi begins to answer, MacNeil interjects, in overlap, the "official" question, "how important is he." (line 18), displaying that the RPQ in lines 10–12 and 14 was not his question, but merely a preface to the question which establishes the context for the question (Heritage 2002a). MacNeil has also designed this RPQ to be understood as an assertion rather than a question by latching onto it, without the small beat of silence that normally comes after a grammatically-complete utterance, a *because* clause (cf. Ford 1993). This *because* clause provides an account for the assertion conveyed in the RPQ, i.e., as if implying "I don't think he'll be able to rally the different elements because, as some people are saying, he is irrelevant, an American puppet." The *really*, especially with its contrastive stress, may also contribute to the question's being heard as an RPQ (cf. Heritage 2002a). MacNeil is able to preserve official neutrality here by the change of footing just prior to the controversial assertion that the former president is "irrelevant, or an american puppet" (lines 12, 14) (cf. Clayman 1992). The RPQ in this case, challenges both Powell's reported speech and Brahimi's position as an Afghan representative who is about to begin talks with the former king about Afghanistan's future. As we see in Brahimi's answer (lines 19–22), he disagrees with this assessment of the former king.

The final example from a broadcast news interview[14] shows that yes/no RPQs done as challenges to a non-present party can also be used affiliatively. In other words, they can challenge non-present parties in order to support or align with co-present parties. This example is taken from a BBC documentary on the history of broadcast televised news interviews. The RPQ here is used in a direct quote, i.e., it is being recalled from past talk rather than transcribed as originally spoken. The speaker, David Frost, in illustrating a past interview style, recalls an interviewer's question which he characterizes as "diffident" and "deferential" rather than "investigative:"

```
(11)   Omnibus
       01 DF:     There was a:: reputed interview
       02         seen after the war: with Anthony
       03         Eden where the interviewer said h
       04         .hh (0.3) u:::h. Mister Eden or Sir
       05         Anthony=whichever 'e was then. .h
       06         (0.1) th::e conservative pa:rty
       07         has been descri:bed as a:: (0.1)
       08         war-mongering pa:rty.=
       09    -->  Is there on:e jot of truth in this
       10    -->  asser:tion? .h No:w, I think
       11         television has become .hh (.) a
       12         little mor::e °hh° .h (.) u::h. h
       13         investigative <th'idea of a little
       14         h> (.) less diffident or
       15         deferential since those days and I
       16         think that's probably healthy,
       17         °.hh° (0.2)
```

The question which Frost quotes, "Is there on:e jot of truth in this asser:tion?" (lines 9–10), is used to challenge an anonymous characterization of the conservative party as a "war-mongering party." This question is seen by Frost as "diffident or deferential"; in other words, it is aligning too strongly with the interviewee. The question may be heard as an RPQ in this example because it contains a strong negative polarity item, *one jot*. *One jot* is one of a class of "minimal unit expressions" such as "not *a soul*," and "didn't lift *a finger*," which either do not occur at all in affirmative statements, or occur with a more literal meaning in such statements (Horn 1978), thus qualifying as negative polarity items. For example, one cannot say (unless with a literal meaning): **There is one jot of truth in this assertion*. That this strong negative polarity item can be used here in a grammatically affirmative question suggests that this question is conveying a negative assertion. The interviewer has just reported a strongly negative description of the interviewee's party as a "war-mongering party" (line 8). He then seems to refute that negative image by asking a question which implies that "there is not one jot of truth in that assertion" (lines 9–10). Thus, Frost characterizes this question as "diffident or deferential".

We have seen how affirmative yes/no RPQs can be used to challenge not only the talk of co-present parties, but also the talk of non-present parties, after bringing that past talk into the current sequence of talk as reported speech. RPQ challenges to talk of non-present parties can be used affiliatively to align with co-present parties, or disaffiliatively, to challenge co-present parties. Although the RPQs in Excerpts 10 and 11 contained items that may facilitate an interpretation of these questions as negative assertions, i.e., *really* in Excerpt 10, and the negative polarity item *one jot* in Excerpt 11, the RPQs in both excerpts were asked by broadcast news interviewers who have institutionally-oriented to claims to knowledge about the questions they are asking. They were thus asked from a position of epistemic strength, as were those in the earlier excerpts.

2.5 Repair initiations used as pre-disagreements

The strong epistemic position from which RPQs are asked can help explain why certain repair initiations can be used as pre-disagreements and can be heard as such by recipients. They do challenging by using a question form to convey assertions of the opposite polarity when the speaker has sufficient epistemic authority. These pre-disagreements can thus be considered a type of yes/no RPQ challenge.

Schegloff (1995b, to appear) discusses how other-initiated repairs can be used as pre-rejections or pre-disagreements, indications that a disagreement is on the way. We have seen examples of this with the "open class" (Drew 1997) repair initiators "huh?" and "pardon me?" in Excerpts 3 and 4. Another form that pre-rejections or pre-disagreements can take is that of a partial repeat of another speaker's previous utterance, with upward intonation (Schegloff 1995b, 1997a, to appear; Schegloff et al. 1977). In the following example, the pro-form "do" (line 4) substitutes for the predicate of the prior utterance, acting like a partial repetition:

```
(12)   TG
       01  Ava:         =B't is wz fun- You sound very
       02                far away.
       03                (0.7)
       04  Bea:   -->   I do?
       05  Ava:          Nyeahm.
       06  Bea:   -->   mNo? I'm no:t,
```

If they are heard as pre-disagreements, these pre-disagreements done as repairs can initiate self-correction (Schegloff et al. 1977) or other types of backdown (Schegloff 1995b, to appear) by targeting a "trouble source" and leaving it for the recipient to correct (Schegloff et al. 1977) or to modify in some way. In this way, pre-disagreements can be used to avoid a dispreferred action, a disagreement, by providing the other party with an opportunity to take action that renders a disagreement unnecessary. The preferred response to a pre-disagreement, done as a repair initiation, is therefore a self-correction, or a backdown, which preempts a dispreferred other-correction or disagreement. In the following example (discussed in Schegloff et al. 1977), Roger's repair initiation "He is?" (line 4) functions as a pre-disagreement. It prompts a backdown from Dan: "Well he was." (line 5), eliminating the necessity for Roger to do an actual disagreement, a dispreferred action:

```
(13)   GTS
       01  Ken:         Is Al there today?
       02  Dan:         Yeah.
       03     -->       (2.0)
       04  Rog:   -->   He is? hh eh heh
       05  Dan:   -->   Well he was.
```

In fact, as in the above example, these repair initiations are often done after a slight gap that maximizes the possibility for a self-correction or backdown to occur in the transition space between speakers after the trouble-source turn (Schegloff 1995b, to appear).

Although each of the above pre-disagreements was done from a strong epistemic position, i.e., the questioner had access to information that would answer the question, only the second engendered a backdown. Even when said from a strong knowledge base, it may not always be clear to the recipient that a disagreement or correction is potentially on the way and that a partial repeat of their prior utterance is not merely a request for confirmation of a hearing. This is exemplified in the following excerpt (discussed in Schegloff et al. 1977):

(14)   **GJ:FN**
```
      ((Three children, Steven, Susan, and Nancy, playing
      water tag; Steven has been tagged, and is now "It"))
      01 Ste:      One, two, three, ((pause)) four
      02           five six ((pause)) eleven eight
      03           nine ten.
      04 Sus: -->  Eleven? eight, nine ten?
      05 Ste: -->  Eleven, eight nine, ten.
      06 Nan: -->  Eleven?
      07 Ste: -->  Seven, eight, nine, ten.
      08 Sus:      That's better.
```

In this excerpt, Steven first responds as if Susan's partial repeat at line 4 is a request for confirmation of a candidate hearing by merely repeating that portion of his prior utterance (line 5). It is not until he gets a second partial repeat from Nancy (line 6), targeting the problem more specifically, that he self-corrects (line 7). Susan's positive evaluation (line 8), shows that she was targeting an error for correction.

This potential for hearing a partial repeat as a request to confirm a hearing, rather than as a pre-disagreement or a prompt for self-correction, will be relevant to the explication of the following disagreement sequence taken from a one-on-one tutoring session held between the teacher and a student as part of a university undergraduate writing course for international students. In this conference, the student, SD, has chosen to work on the second draft of his paper in which he discusses Charles de Gaulle's leadership, using various theories of leadership from class readings. The pedagogical focus of this sequence is on learning what is relevant to include from outside sources. Prior to this excerpt, SD has already established that he will be discussing Charles de Gaulle in terms of Zaleznik's (1984) concept of *charismatic leadership* and Gardner's (1996) concept of *direct leadership*. In this excerpt the teacher, TC, begins by criticizing SD's inclusion of leadership terminology that will not be relevant to his thesis. SD accounts for including this terminology by characterizing it as "background." TC challenges SD's characterization of this material as background with a pre-disagreement done as a partial repeat of the prior utterance. A copy of the relevant portion of the student's paper (italics added) is provided as Excerpt 15, prior to the transcript, Excerpt 16.

(15) **SD Text**
    Leadership is rarely discovered in individuals. That is why we look upon persons who have been known to possess the leadership. And we have often been influenced by their words, actions, and their philosophy. We are influenced by the leaders because in their words or story we find common goals or solutions that we seek to solve for certain problems.

    According to Gardner, these leaders are categorized as direct, indirect, ordinary, innovative or visionary leaders. However, Zaleznik differentiates the leaders as either charismatic or consensus. On the other hand Wills defines a leader as a person who 'mobilizes others toward a goal shared by leader and followers.' With these various explanations about the leadership, I think of a person who became my mentor, who is Charles de Gaulle of France. Charles de Gaulle does not possess every leadership the three authors discuss. But he successfully tells his story and embodies his story well that people become able to learn from him.

(16) **TC/SD:7**

```
61 TC:15      ok. ((reading)) "according to de
62            Gaulle" ((she meant "Gardner"))
63            ↓here's what you say "according
64            to de Gaulle leaders are char-
65            categorized as direct indirect
66            (0.2) ordinary innovative (0.8)
67            or: visionary."↓
68            (1.5) ((TC eyegaze on text;
69            bent over text))
70            why did you: talk about that.
71            (0.8) ((TC moves paper toward SD;
72            straightens body;
73            eyegaze still on text))
74 SD:        uh s- [cause (0.8) d- this one of
75                  [((TC looks up briefly at
76            SD, then down at text))
77            the sources that we (.) read in
78            cla[ss.
79 TC:           [um [hum?
80 SD:              [so I jus wanted ta include
81            that. as uh: information.
82            (0.5) ((TC eyegaze on SD))
83 TC:        Is it relevant?
84            *to what you're saying?
85            (0.8)* ((*SD looks down))
86 SD:        No it's just background. heh h
87 TC:   --> It's background?=
```

```
88  SD:    =yeah.=
89  TC:    ok how's it background.=because I-
90         like .h most people wouldn't
91         know[:
92  SD:         [((sniff))
93  TC:    maybe what he meant by direct
94         indirect ordinary innovative or
95         visionary.
96  SD:    (yeah.)/(well) ok,
97         (1.5) ((SD nods))
```

Excerpt 16 begins as TC reads aloud the first sentence of SD's second paragraph which introduces, without explanation, not only Gardener's category of "direct leadership" but the categories of "indirect, ordinary, innovative, and visionary," none of which SD is applying to his discussion of de Gaulle (lines 61–67). TC then continues to silently direct her attention to the text, with eyegaze (lines 68–69), possibly demonstrating something problematic in the text. TC breaks the silence by posing a question which asks SD to justify why he included this information in his text, "why did you: talk about that." (line 70). In her request for justification, TC puts contrastive stress on "that", contrasting what she has just read in SD's text (direct, indirect, ordinary, innovative and visionary) with what SD has just claimed (prior to this excerpt) were the two theories of leadership he was discussing in his essay: *charismatic leadership* and *direct leadership*. This request for a justification can already, at this point, let the student know that the teacher sees this portion of the essay as problematic. When an expert asks a novice to justify an action, this makes the action accountable (cf. Sacks 1992 [1964/1965]) and can suggest that there is something problematic with that action, especially in a setting where the goal is to discuss how to improve a performance.

SD gives a justification for including this information in his text (lines 74, 77–78, 80–81), but only after a .8 second pause: "uh s- cause (0.8) d- this one of the sources that we (.) read in class. so I jus wanted ta include that. as uh: information." The prior .8 second pause, and the .8 second pause shortly after he begins (line 74), can show an orientation to his justification as a dispreferred, or non-aligning response (Pomerantz 1978, 1984; Sacks 1987 [1973]; Schegloff 1995b, to appear), demonstrating that he sees TC's question as suggesting the text is problematic.[16] SD's justification also shows that he may be treating this essay as if it were an essay exam to test his knowledge of the sources for this essay. SD's interpretation is understandable since probably most, if not all, of his previous writing in school has been for the purpose of showing the teacher what he has learned from the lectures and the reading.

TC then asks a question which elicits a mixed response from SD:

```
83 TC:   Is it relevant?
84       *to what you're saying?
85       (0.8)* ((*SD looks down))
86 SD:   No it's just background. heh h
```

There are two issues involved here. One is that SD has introduced many leadership categories from Gardner, "direct, indirect, ordinary, innovative, and visionary"; however, only the first category, *direct*, is relevant to his essay on de Gaulle. The second issue is one of *recipient design* (Sacks et al. 1974): SD has introduced the terms without defining them, as if writing for the teacher or other members of his class. Although the teacher may in fact be the only other person who will read this essay, except for possibly a few other class members, it becomes clear later that this paper is meant to be written for an abstract academic audience who are not necessarily familiar with the class readings.[17]

When TC asks, "Is it relevant? to what you're saying?" (lines 83–84), in a context where both TC and SD have already discussed the fact that most of these characteristics of leadership are not relevant, this question, like the yes-no questions discussed above, conveys a strong negative assertion (see Chapter 4, for a more complete discussion of similar yes/no questions in pedagogy). TC seems to be reminding SD that this information is not relevant to what SD has just agreed he was focusing on in his paper.

SD agrees with the teacher's criticism that what he has written is not relevant to what he is saying about de Gaulle. His "no" (line 86) aligns with the negative assertion implied by TC, "It's not relevant to what you're saying."[18] However, this negative assertion, which shows why that portion of text is problematic, also implies a solution, provided that the student is familiar with the norms of American academic written discourse being oriented to here, i.e., "If it's not relevant, it should be removed from the text." SD does not seem to agree with the implication that the irrelevant leadership characteristics should be eliminated. He adds an utterance which suggests he had some proper reasons for including this information: "it's just background. heh h" (line 86). He displays his agreement with TC's implied criticism by using the word *just*, i.e., it's not relevant to what he's saying about de Gaulle; it's *merely* background. The short laugh token also may imply an agreement with the teacher's criticism. Throughout the conference, SD produces similar short laugh tokens at places in the interaction that could be potentially embarrassing for him. Here he could be demonstrating embarrassment at having an obvious lack of relevance pointed out to him. However, SD does not appear to agree with or understand the implied solution: that the information should be eliminated. He seems to be justifying its inclusion as "background." This is understandable since probably most, if not all, of his previous writing in school has been for the purpose of showing the teacher what he has learned from the lectures and the reading. From his perspective, if he is to show what he knows, to demonstrate his familiarity with the readings, there is no better place to put this demonstration than in the introductory paragraph before his thesis statement, and the only way to characterize it would be as general *background*, even though it is not relevant to what he will later say about de Gaulle.

Background in this type of essay, however, is normally thought of as information that will help the reader understand some portion of the text. SD's assertion that "it's just background" brings up the second problem with the information in SD's text: he has introduced the terms without defining them for the reader. TC chooses to deal with this issue before returning to the issue of relevance. She challenges SD's assertion with the following question: "It's background?" (line 87). Like Joseph's first RPQ in Excerpt 8, this question is a grammatically affirmative *declarative question* (Quirk et al. 1985; Weber 1993) with upward intonation. To the extent that it is heard as a candidate hearing of SD's turn, proffered to SD for confirmation, it would prefer a *yes* answer. However, the teacher seems to be using this question not to confirm her hearing – there is no evidence of anything in the immediate context that would lead to trouble in hearing or understanding what the student had said[19] – but as a pre-disagreement, questioning the student's previous assertion, and implying that she does not consider it background. This becomes evident as the talk unfolds. As will be seen, she follows with talk that challenges the student's characterization of this portion of text as background.

As a pre-disagreement that questions the student's characterization of his text, "It's background?" conveys an assertion of the opposite polarity, a negative assertion, i.e., "It's not background." It would therefore be a type of RPQ. It uses, as discussed above, the mechanism of repair, taking a form common to both candidate hearings and pre-disagreements (Schegloff 1995b, 1997a, to appear; Schegloff et al. 1977): a partial repetition of the prior utterance with upward intonation. It is followed by the actual disagreement (lines 89–91, 93–95), discussed in more detail in Chapter 3.

Using an RPQ that does a partial repeat of another's previous utterance as the first element in a pre-disagreement sequence has an advantage. Because the RPQ allows the questioner to convey an assertion "off the record," and avoid responsibility for making that assertion, it allows the possibility of a disagreement to be suggested, and, if that possibility is registered by the recipient, it allows the recipient to do a backdown, removing the need to do the actual disagreement, which would be a dispreferred action.

However, speakers who do a pre-sequence, such as a pre-disagreement, in order to avoid doing a dispreferred action, such as a disagreement, may face a problem. Their recipients may not be aware that they are being prompted to perform a particular action, such as a backdown (Schegloff 1995b, to appear). Alternatively, recipients may be aware of what is being asked of them, but they may choose to avoid this action. In Excerpt 16 above, SD does not treat TC's "It's background?" as a pre-disagreement. He could not, of course, do a self-correction if he did not yet know what the problem was with his characterization of this portion of text as background. But he could, on sensing a possible disagreement, choose to do a backdown, weakening the epistemic claim of his assertion, for example "Isn't it?", as was done by Rich and Wes in Excerpts 3 and 4 respectively. However, by producing an affirmative response in a preferred manner, a response which does not align with the implied assertion in the pre-disagreement, SD treats this partial repetition as a simple request for confirmation of what he has just said rather than as a pre-disagreement:

```
87 TC:      It's background?=
88 SD: -->  =yeah.=
```

In this example, it is possible that SD does not treat this turn as a pre-disagreement because it is equivocal who has the greater claim to knowledge here, the student or the teacher. From the student's perspective, he does, as he is giving an explanation for why he included certain material in his essay. From the teacher's perspective, however, it is her status as expert that prompts her to question the student's definition of the term *background* displayed in his response.

In the next pedagogical example, however, it is clear to the students that the repair initiation is being used to elicit an error correction. Teachers, especially language teachers, make use of a partial repetition of a student's prior incorrect utterance to initiate repair on that utterance in order to give the student the opportunity to self-correct. After a student provides an answer to a *test* (Searle 1969) or *known information* (Mehan 1979b) question, one to which the teacher already knows the answer, there is an expectation that the teacher will evaluate that answer in the third turn (Mehan 1979b). Thus if a teacher initiates repair on a student's answer by repeating it with upward intonation, the teacher's epistemic authority, together with the fact that this repair appears in the *evaluation* position, will often convey to students that their answer was problematic. Teachers can thus use this practice to elicit self-correction. The following example is taken from an English as a Second Language (ESL) reading class. The teacher has just defined the idiom *bringing home the bacon* and is checking to see if the students, predominately Koreans, understand it by asking them a question within their domain of knowledge:

(17)   MGLIT 7/18/00
```
01  TM:         in korea who- who usually brings
02              home the bacon. men or women.
03  S?:         (      )
04  S4?:        uh men.
05  S1:         men.
06  S4:    -->  daught[ers.
07  S?:               [°daughter.°
08  TM:    -->  daughters:
09  S?:         huh huh [huh hhh
10  SS:                 [hhhhhhh
11  S4:    -->  father.
12  TM:         yeah. yeah. the father. the the
13              husband usually brings home the
14              bacon. al[right,=
```

After one student, S4, uses an incorrect lexical item, "daughters" (line 6), in response to the teacher's *test* question, the teacher questions this term (line 8) by repeating it with additional stress and exaggerated upward intonation (indicated by the underlined colon). This repair initiation elicits a correction from the student (line 11). In this example, the fact that the teacher's repair initiation was done with unusual prosody in the evaluation turn after a student's answer, and the laughter of other students, all could have helped to bring to the student's attention an error that she was able to correct herself.

We have seen that certain repair initiations, done as partial or full repeats of a prior turn with upward intonation, can be understood as RPQs, and thus as pre-disagreements, partly because of the strong knowledge base from which they are asked. But because they are done as repair initiations, they can also be confused with candidate hearings proffered for confirmation. However, when these repair initiations are accompanied by additional stress and laughter, as in Excerpts 13 and 17, the stress and laughter may call attention to the error. Pedagogical repair initiations made in the third turn after a *known-information* or *test* question may be especially vulnerable to being heard as pre-disagreements because this is the turn in which the teacher's evaluation of the answer normally occurs.

2.6 Summary and discussion

In this chapter we have seen how certain yes/no questions can convey strong reversed polarity assertions, thereby conveying the epistemic stance of the speaker. I have called these questions *reversed polarity questions*, or RPQs. Because these questions convey strong assertions, they are *conducive*, and carry a *preference* for a certain answer, one that agrees with the stance of the speaker. Dispreferred answers are thus heard as disagreements.

These questions are regularly used in a variety of disaffiliative actions that challenge prior talk or actions. Grammatically negative yes/no questions, when asked by interviewers, are regularly heard as accusations of interviewees. Grammatically affirmative yes/no questions can be used to accuse, to defend oneself against an accusation, to sanction children, or, as repair initiations, to point out errors and elicit self-correction. Yes/no RPQs can also be used to challenge the reported speech of non-present third parties in order to align with or to challenge co-present parties.

Some yes/no RPQs may contain items such as *really* and *one jot*, as in Excerpts 10 and 11, contrastive stress, as in Excerpts 8–10, or the exaggerated intonation and accompanying laughter of the repair initiations in Excerpts 13 and 17, that can facilitate an interpretation as negative assertions. However, other yes/no RPQs contain nothing in their design that distinguishes them from ordinary information-seeking questions. Many of these questions, isolated from their interactional contexts, could be heard as *asking a question*, i.e., seeking information, rather than *questioning* a prior utterance or action. How are they heard as *questioning*, i.e., as asserting opinions that challenge a prior utterance or action? Both the displayed knowledge state of the questioner and the question's position in a particular course of action can help determine whether the question is heard as an RPQ or as an ordinary, information-seeking question. Yes/no RPQs are more likely to be heard as challenges when they are asked from the position of epistemic strength. Either the speakers have institutionally-oriented to claims to knowledge about the questions they are asking, as do broadcast news interviewers and teachers, or the question is asking about something already displayed to be in the speaker's knowledge domain. Aside from epistemic strength, the sequential position of the questions can also contribute to their being heard as RPQs. They are more likely to be heard as challenges, rather than as information-seeking questions, when challenges would be expected responses, e.g., after accusations. And when they are used to initiate repair in pedagogical situations after students' answers to *known-answer* questions, they are more likely to be heard as *pre-disagreements* because it is at that point that students are led to expect evaluations of their answers.

Many of the questions described in this chapter would ordinarily be labeled *rhetorical questions*. I have used the term *reversed polarity question*, or *RPQ*, rather than *rhetorical question*, for two reasons. First, the term *rhetorical question* may suggest that these questions do not receive answers. Although these questions can receive outright disagreements as in Excerpts 5 ("I disagree with that,") and 6 ("I do not agree with you…"), many yes/no RPQs do, in fact, receive *yes* or *no* answers. What these questions have in common is that they are heard as asserting opinions rather than as seeking information. Answers are therefore done to either align or disalign with the opinion conveyed through the question. Second, the term *RPQ* allows us to capture the clear relationship between those questions that are commonly thought of as *rhetorical* and similar *reversed polarity questions* used as repair initiations to elicit self-corrections. As suggested above, the relationship between these types of questions can be characterized by the verb *question*, as in "question a prior utterance or action," as opposed to *asking a question*, i.e., asking for information. Both types of RPQs are used to *question*, i.e., they convey opinions that challenge a prior utterance or action.

CHAPTER 3

Wh- reversed polarity questions

3.1 Introduction

In the previous chapter we looked at yes/no RPQs used as challenges. This chapter describes similar RPQs that are grammatically formatted as wh-questions, e.g.:

(18)
```
when have I.
so an ↑when other time have I ever done that↑
ok how's it background.
how are we vulnerable
```

Here is a clear example in its interactional context, which I will later explicate more fully. Two friends, Debbie and Shelley, are having an argument. Debbie has accused Shelley of pulling out of an upcoming trip together because her boyfriend cannot go. The focal utterance is "when have I." (line 40):

(19) **Debbie and Shelley**
```
35 Deb:      =I do'know,=jus don't blow off
36           your girlfriends for guy:s,
37           Shel.
38 Shel:     De:b I'm not. h[ow man-]e-
39 Deb:                     [o ka:y ]
40 Shel: --> when have I.=beside ya- I mean
```

As with the yes/no RPQs, these wh-questions are not treated by the participants as information-seeking questions. Sometimes they are not even designed to make answers relevant, i.e., speakers do not always stop to allow for answers to be given. These questions are treated by both speakers and recipients as challenges to prior utterances or actions. Like the yes/no RPQs, these wh-questions can be used as challenges because they convey a strong epistemic stance of the questioner, specifically a negative assertion. In other words, the stance expressed is that of the corresponding negative statement; "when have I." implies "never have I", or "I never have."

Like the yes/no RPQs, wh-questions are likely to be heard as RPQs when the question is asked from a position of epistemic strength, i.e., the question is asking about something in the questioner's knowledge domain. But, as we will see, their position in a sequence of action is even more important in determining how wh-question RPQs are interpreted. They occur in an already-established environment of disagreement, accusation, complaint, and the like, where challenging is a sequentially appropriate next response.

Like many of the reversed polarity yes/no questions described earlier, these wh-questions have traditionally been categorized as *rhetorical questions*. In describing these questions, some linguists, e.g., Bolinger (1957), Horn (1978) and Quirk et al. (1985) have also noted their ability to convey strong negative assertions. Bolinger (1957) categorizes rhetorical questions as sub-group of conducive wh-questions, i.e., wh-questions which display an expectation for a certain answer. According to Bolinger, these questions are either "uttered in a context which cancels certain otherwise possible answers," as in "'Look, it's John who just came in.' – 'Who else?'" (157) or they contain expressions, such as those indicating undesirability, which make the question conducive, e.g., "Who believes such *nonsense?*" (158). Bolinger claims that "the answer expected is some synonym of 'zero': *nobody, nothing, nowhere, none, no reason*, etc." (157). Horn (1978: 151), listing "non-overtly negative environments" which allow negative polarity items, such as *ever* and *lift a finger*, mentions questions such as "Who would lift a finger for you?" and "When has he ever said a word against his mother?" In such questions, according to Horn, "the stance expressed by the questioner is clearly that of the corresponding negatives: no one, and never." Quirk et al. (1985:826) also discuss grammatically affirmative wh-questions which are "equivalent to a statement in which the wh- element is replaced by a negative element," e.g.:

> Who knows/cares? ['Nobody knows/cares' or "I don't know/care.']
> What difference does it make? ['It makes no difference.']
> How should I know? ['There is no reason why I should know.']

However, this literature on the whole gives us no way of understanding, in particular social interactional contexts, how wh-questions that do not contain either "expressions indicating undesirability" or negative polarity items come to be understood as expressing assertions; nor does it discuss what actions participants can use these questions to accomplish. In this chapter I examine several contexts where such questions are used to challenge prior utterances or actions. I show how the wh-questions come to be heard as asserting a strong stance toward a prior utterance or action, and how this hearing enables the questions to be used to challenge that prior utterance or action.

3.2 Wh-questions used to challenge co-present parties

We will now return to the telephone conversation between Debbie and Shelley, from which Excerpt 19 was taken. In this conversation, Debbie makes two different types of accusations against Shelley. The first concerns the reason why Shelley canceled her plans to participate in an upcoming trip. Debbie accuses Shelley of canceling because her boyfriend, Mark, is unable to go. The second accusation is more serious. Debbie suggests that Shelley's behavior on this occasion is part of a larger pattern. It is this second accusation that Shelley challenges with a series of three similar wh-questions, shown in the following three excerpts. In Excerpt 20 below, the wh-question (line 40) is used to challenge an implication by Debbie, in the prior turn, that Shelley "blows off her girlfriends for guys":

(20) **Debbie and Shelley**

```
03   Deb:      ↑[I↑ just don want you do it jus
04             because Marks not going.=cause
05             th[at's just
06   Shel:       [Oh I know.=
07   Deb:      =that .h
08   Shel:     >°I know°<=
09   Deb:      =it's jus' like you- yaknow:, if
10             you don't wanta do something
11             with like a gi:rlfriend
12             jus cause this guy:s not
13             goin[g it] would piss me o:ff.
14   Shel:         [no:.]
15   Shel:     give me a break.
16   Deb:      ↑well Shelley, that's how it
17             sou::nds,↑ =
18   Shel:     =w'll a-=
19   Deb:      =I mean I'm jus telling you how
20             it sou:[nds.
21   Shel:            [I understand that but ya
22             I- I mean it's not- it's not just
23             tha:t I mean IwaIw I was excited
24             to go befor:e, and I still wanna
25             go, its jus I mean I don't wanna
```

```
26              spend the money: and I know I
27              have other responsibiliti:es:=
28              an,=
29  Deb:        =but if- but th- see this is
30              what I'm see:in. I'm seein well:
31              that's okay, but if Mark went you
32              would spend the mo::ney.
33  Shel:       ↑°no:, that's not true↑ either.=
34              ((begins soft, then rising))
35  Deb:        =I do'know,=jus don't blow off
36              your girlfriends for guy:s,
37              Shel.
38  Shel:       De:b I'm not. h[ow man-]e-
39  Deb:                       [o ka:y ]
40  Shel:  -->  when have I.=beside ya- I mean
41              I mean you're right a- it w's
42              easier w- with him going
43              because he was going to pay f-
44              for a lot of it.=b[ut]
45  Deb:                         [ye]ah,=
46  Shel:       =that's no:t .h >I mean< that's
47              not thee reason I'm not going.
48  Deb:        mmkay,
```

Through a series of turns, Debbie suggests a possible account for why Shelley is not going on the trip as planned. She implies that it's because Mark is not going. In lines 3–4 Debbie suggests that this is not a valid reason for pulling out of the trip, implying that it *was* the reason. She makes the same implication again in lines 9–13, further implying that Shelley does not properly value her relationship with a girlfriend, i.e., Debbie. And in lines 29–32, Debbie again implies that Shelley canceled because Mark wasn't going, rejecting Shelley's account that she didn't want to spend the money. Debbie presents her account as an accusation, as an account that is not justified (lines 3–4) and that, if true, "would piss [her] o:ff" (line 13). Over the course of the talk, Shelley repeatedly denies Debbie's account (lines 14, 22–23, 33, 38, 46–47) and gives an alternate account (lines 23–27, 41–44), that she didn't want to spend that much money now that Mark is not going and not paying part of her share.

The above accusation concerns the reason for withdrawing from this particular trip. In the course of the talk, however, Debbie makes a more serious accusation, i.e., that this type of behavior is typical of Shelley. She makes this accusation implicitly in lines 35–37 when she says "jus don't blow off your girlfriends for guy:s, Shel." By admonishing Shelley not to "blow off your girlfriends for guy:s," Debbie not only implies that this is what Shelley has been doing in this particular instance, but that Shelley has done this before. She implies this by pluralizing both "girlfriends" and "guys."

In answer to Debbie's accusation that Shelley is "blowing off her girlfriends for guys", Shelley first denies the accusation in relation to this particular instance, "De:b I'm not." (line 38). Following this, she begins and quickly abandons a question that seems as though it may have been heading towards something like "how many times have I done that." (line 38). She then asks another question, "when have I." (line 40). As I will show, neither the abandoned question nor the completed question is asking for information; both are examples of wh-questions used to convey negative assertions. With her second, completed question, "when have I.", Shelley seems to be challenging Debbie's broader accusation that this behavior is typical by implying that she has never been guilty of "blowing off her girlfriends for guys." The question "when have I." thus implies "I never have."

How does Shelley's utterance, "when have I.", come to be understood as a negative assertion? As explained earlier, participants in conversation interpret utterances based on their understanding of what preceded those utterances and the course of action that the preceding utterances seem to be implementing. They ask the question: "Why that now?" (Schegloff & Sacks 1973). Shelley's utterance occurs in a challenge environment, after Shelley is accused of "blowing off her girlfriends for guys", and after Shelley explicitly denies this accusation in relation to the current incident, "De:b I'm not." In this sequential position, a request for Debbie to provide Shelley with new information about the times she has done something Shelley has just denied doing would make no sense. However, an utterance implying that Shelley has *never* "blown off girlfriends for guys" would be a sequentially appropriate challenge to Debbie's accusation. Thus, the question's sequential position provides a key to its interpretation as a negative assertion.

By means of its adjacent positioning in the next turn, this question refers anaphorically back to the assumption underlying Debbie's prior turn, i.e., that Shelley has blown off girlfriends for guys, challenging that assumption. It does this challenge by implying that Debbie will not be able to name a particular instance of this behavior to give an account for her accusation because Shelley has never been guilty of this behavior. The implication is that the question is unanswerable and thus Debbie's accusation cannot be supported.

Shelley designs the continuation of her turn in a way that does not invite an answer to the question, displaying her orientation to the question as doing challenging, rather than asking for information. She rushes through the end of that question, without the beat of silence normally found at a transition relevance place, into further talk that deals with her reasons for withdrawing from this particular trip (lines 40–44). Thus, both the interactional context of the question and the design of the turn in which it is uttered facilitate an understanding of the question as not asking for information but rather doing challenging by negating a prior assertion.

An understanding of Shelley's utterance, "when have I.", as conveying a negative assertion, i.e., "I never have", also explains Shelley's self-repair in line 38. If Shelley's cut-off turn constructional unit (TCU), "how man-" was, in fact, headed towards "how many times have I done that", conveying a similar negative assertion, Shelley would have implied that there were not many times when she had "blown off her girlfriends for guys." Her repair upgrades the claim to imply that she has never done this, that Debbie would not be able to name a single instance, and that therefore Debbie's accusation is untenable.[20]

Several turns later Debbie utters an accusation similar to the one in lines 35–37, implying that this behavior is typical for Shelley (lines 15–18 below), and Shelley responds with a similar wh-question, "when."

(21) **Debbie and Shelley**

```
12  Shel:         alright,
13                [well don get ma:[d at me.
14  Deb:          [.hh             [.HH I'M NOT
15                MA:D but it jus seems like
16                it's like you can't do
17                anything unless there's a
18                gu:y involved an' it jus
19                pisses me o- >I'm jus bein
20                rea:l ho:nest with ya cuz its
21                like=.hh[h  [why wouldn:t- =
22  Shel:  -->            [whe[n.
23  Deb:          =why wouldn't you go.=becu:z
24                I mean (.) that's what Jay Tee
25                told me you told hi:m,
26  Shel:         w'll that's what- when I
27                called him I told him that I
28                didn't have the money or that
29                he- Mark can't go becu:z o:f
30                work.
31  Deb:          mmh[m
32  Shel:            [that's why he can't go..hh
33                an I said b-to be real honest
34                with you: I have to decide do
```

```
35              I wanna spend this money
36              becuz if Mark was goin .hh he
37              was gonna pay fer- fer m- a
38              lot of it.=cause he won money
39              playing footba:ll.
40   Deb:       uhuh
41   Shel:      So: it w's like awright
42              fi:ne.=I'll let you: buy my-
43              my plane ticket, that's not a
44              problem, [.hh a]n: now=
45   Deb:                [uhuh ]
46   Shel:      =that he's not going, I have
47              to pay for the whole thing
48              an: that's fi:ne,=except for:
49              .hh yaknow I have my sister
50              comin in an stuff an I'm like
51              well do I wreally wanna do this?
52              well yeah I wanna do it, but
53              do I have the money to do:
54              [all the]se things.=
55   Deb:       [ri:ght.]
56   Deb:       =okay ((high pitch))
```

Shelley's "when." (line 22) again uses adjacency, i.e., positioning in the next turn, to refer back to Debbie's accusation that "you can't do anything unless there's a gu:y involved." It does not immediately follow the accusation, but occurs somewhat interruptively later into Debbie's turn, possibly because Debbie has not given Shelley a chance to respond; she has rushed through several possible turn transition points (lines 18–21) after the accusation. Shelley's "when.", like her earlier "when have I.", challenges Debbie's claim that this behavior is typical by implying that Shelley never has been guilty of this behavior; Debbie would not be able to name a particular instance of it. Possibly because it occurs at a point where turn transition is not relevant, Shelly's "when." is not responded to.

After re-explaining her reasons for withdrawing from the upcoming trip (lines 26–30, 32–39, 41–44, 46–54), providing an alternate account to Debbie's, Shelley again explicitly denies Debbie's account and summarizes her own account of why she pulled out of the upcoming trip (lines 57–60 below). She then deals with Debbie's broader accusation that this behavior is typical by reissuing the question asked in Excerpt 21, line 22, reformulating it (lines 62–63):

(22) **Debbie and Shelley**
```
57  Shel:      So: I mean it's not becuz hes-
58             hes- I mean it's not becuz he:s
59             not going its becuz (0.5) his
60             money's not (0.5) funding me.
61  Deb:       okay,
62  Shel: -->  So an ↑when other time have
63        -->  I ever [done that↑  ]
64             ((higher pitch on "that"))
65  Deb:              [.hhh ↑ well ]I'm jus
66             sayin ↑ it jus seems you-
67             you base a lot of things on-on
68             guy:s.(·) I do'know:, it just- a
69             couple times I don- I don- .hh
70             it's not a big deal.
71             (·)
72  Deb:       it's [rea:lly.   ]
73  Shel:           [°↓that's no]t true
74             Debbie↓[the onl-] the only=
75  Deb:              [ its not]
76  Shel:      =time I d- n-now your talkin
77             about like (·) me not goin to
78             your party because of Jay, an
79             you're right.=that was becuz of
80             him.=.hh and that wuz pro[bly
81  Deb:                                [↑NO I
82             understood tha:t, I don' care
83             'bout tha:t.=
```

Shelley's question, "So an ↑when other time have I ever done that↑", (lines 62–63) is likely a conflation of "what other time have I ever done that" and "when have I ever done that." Like the previous question "when." (Excerpt 21, line 22), it seems to imply that she has *not* been guilty of Debbie's broader accusation that she "can't do anything unless there's a guy involved."[21] This version of the question is specifically built to deal with the accusation involving "other" times Shelley has been supposedly guilty of this behavior. As with the previous questions, this one refers anaphorically back to the claim it is challenging; however, perhaps because it is not positioned in the next turn after the accusation and cannot rely on adjacent positioning, this question uses substitution with the pro-forms "do that" (Halliday & Hasan 1976) to refer back to Debbie's accusation. As in Excerpt 20, Shelley seems to be challenging Debbie by implying that she will not be able to provide an instance of the behavior she has been accused of and that she has never been guilty of this behavior.

Because these questions are treated by the questioner as unanswerable, it does not mean that they are never answered. As we have seen in Excerpt 20, questioners can make answers difficult to do by rushing through the end of the question into their next utterance. However, in Excerpt 22, Debbie takes a turn even before Shelley's question is finished, and during the course of that turn, Debbie answers Shelley's wh-question with "a couple times", i.e., ".hhh ↑ well I'm jus sayin ↑ it jus seems you- you base a lot of things on-on gu:y:s.(·) I do'know:, it just- a couple times I don- I don- .hh it's not a big deal." (lines 65–70). However, in her answer, Debbie displays an orientation to Shelley's question as doing a challenge, and thus, as conveying an assertion. Her answer to the "when" question is delayed well into her turn. She begins her turn by first addressing Shelley's challenge, doing her answer as a backdown. Debbie weakens her earlier claim that Shelley "can't do anything unless there's a gu:y involved", to "↑well I'm jus sayin↑ it jus seems you- you base a lot of things on-on gu:y:s." The turn is highly mitigated, with "well", "just", and "seems". When she does answer the "when" question, her answer contrasts with her earlier implication that this behavior has been typical for Shelley. She now claims that Shelley has done this "a couple times", mitigating her claim with "I do'know:," and "it's not a big deal." Even though the turn in which this answer is incorporated is done as a backdown, and even though Shelley later concedes that she may have exhibited one instance of this behavior (lines 74, 76–80), Shelley first clearly denies that she has exhibited this behavior even "a couple times": "° ↓that's not true Debbie↓" (lines 73–74). This denial shows that her wh-question, "So an ↑when other time have I ever done that↑" (lines 62–63), was used to convey a negative assertion, displaying a stance that challenged Debbie's accusation.

In an excerpt from a different telephone call, a wh-question challenge is also answered by the recipient, but it is similarly made clear in the interaction that the question is being used as a challenge, and that the questioner is treating it as unanswerable. Mark has called his friend Bob to complain about not having been informed about an upcoming party at Bob's place. The excerpt begins with Bob's account for why Mark had not been informed:

(23)²² **SF2**

```
01  BOB:    Ma:rk yihknow what the deal
02          i:s˙hh Yer jist uh::hhh ˙hhhhhh
03          Yer outta circulation here.hhh
04          (0.2)
05  BOB:    [( )
06  MAR:    [Whadidja mea:::n ˙hhhh-hhh
```

```
07              (0.3)
08  BOB:        Well yih .tch! (0.4) Cuz we
09              always yihknow we take fer
10              grannid thet you know these
11              things.
12  MAR:        [Uh huh.
13  BOB:        [˙hhhhh 'tchu:'ve uh: gone outta
14              circulation you: don't pick these
15              things u:p.=
16  MAR:        =hhhhh=
17  BOB:        =Yihknow,
18  MAR:    --> Wu:ll where wz I spozetuh pick
19          --> this stuff up at. 'n I'm
20  MAR:        [not out'v]circulation, ]
21  BOB:        [O h : a ]football game ]
22              'er::(s)-
23  ???:        ˙k ˙hhhh
24  MAR:        We:ll I wen't'the football ga:me?
25              (·)
26  BOB:        en nobuddy told you (    [        )
27  MAR:                                 [˙hhhhhhh
28  MAR:        en no one mentioned a word.hh
29              (·)
30  BOB:        Mark,hh (0.3) will you come to a
31              party Fridee hmhhuh huh huh huh
32              huh
```

Bob accounts for Mark's not having been informed about the party by claiming that he and his friends always take for granted that Mark will hear about upcoming social gatherings, i.e., without a specific effort at informing him, but because Mark has been "outta circulation" (line 3), he hasn't heard about this party. This account is then a counter-accusation, challenging Mark's earlier accusation. Bob is claiming that if Mark hadn't been out of circulation, he would have heard about the party. Mark challenges this account in two ways. First, with a wh-question challenge, "Wu:ll where wz I spozetuh pick this stuff up at" (lines 18–19), he implies that there was no place he could have heard (i.e., incidentally, without a specific effort to inform him) about the upcoming party, and second, in denying that he has been out of circulation (lines 19–20), he implies that he has made himself available to be informed incidentally. In overlap with Mark, Bob answers the wh-question, giving an example of the type of place Mark could have heard about the party, i.e., a football game (line 21). Mark challenges that example, and thus, the implication that there was an occasion when he could have heard about the party, by saying that he had attended the football game (line 24). Bob subsequently makes the implication of Mark's utterance explicit by adding to Mark's prior utterance: "en nobuddy told you ..." (line 26), an inference which is not only confirmed by Mark but intensified ("en no one mentioned *a word*", line 28). In implying, and then confirming, that he hadn't heard about the party at the football game, Mark is again conveying the stance that his wh-question (lines 18–19) is unanswerable, i.e., there was nowhere he could have heard incidentally about the upcoming party without being specifically invited. Bob's account for not having specifically invited him is thus inadequate. Bob aligns with this position by making the implication of Mark's utterance explicit in line 26, and by jokingly issuing a "formal" invitation (lines 30–32), a remedy for Mark's original complaint.

The above wh-questions are all used to challenge accusations made by co-present parties. They ask the accuser to provide support for the accusation, and, at the same time, imply that no support can be found and that the accusation is thus untenable.

3.3 Wh-questions used to challenge non-present parties

As with yes/no question challenges, wh- RPQs can also be used to challenge non-present parties. In the analysis of wh-question challenges to non-present parties, we will also see how these questions can be used to challenge reported actions as well as prior talk.

Clayman (2002) suggests that *how* questions may be especially vulnerable to being heard as unanswerable. Although *how* questions in my data can be heard as ordinary information-seeking questions, it may be that the form *how can* (+ *pronoun*) is especially vulnerable to being heard as a canonical challenge. I discuss canonical wh-question challenges in more detail later in this chapter.

The *how can* question in the following example, discussed by Clayman (2002), is used to align with a co-present party by challenging a non-present party. In this way, it is similar to the yes/no RPQ discussed in Excerpt 11, Chapter 2: "Is there on:e jot of truth in this asser:tion?". The excerpt is taken from a phone call between two young women, Hyla and Nancy, in the mid 1970's. Hyla is telling her friend Nancy about a "Dear Abby" advice column where a fifteen-year-old girl complains that her mother will not let her wear revealing clothing. Hyla is upset that Abby agrees with the mother. This is the second story where Hyla recounts what she calls Abby's "stupid" advice to a young girl. Nancy uses a wh-question (line 24) to challenge Abby's advice, aligning with Hyla's stance.

(24) [HGII: 18–19]
```
01  Hyl:      =eh-eh .he:::hhh Yesterday, (.)
02            wa:s, .hhh this gi:rl, .hh °e-
03            fifteen year old girl her mother
04            didn' let'er wear sho:rt skirts 'r
05            midriff to[:ps'r h]alter to:::ps'r=
06  Nan:            [Uh hu:h]
07  Hyl:      =e::nnything,=
08  Nan:      =[Yea:h,
09  Hyl:      =[.hh Y' know specially some(h)ing
10            thet'd sh-w'd show her navel,.hhhhh
11            [A : : n : : d,]=
12  Nan:      [°°hhhh Ghhhod.]=
13  Hyl:      =En Abby agreed thet you don't,
14            i:t- thet it's jist invhhiting
15            trouble.=
16  Nan:      =Oh:::-::::.
17            (.)
18  Hyl:      .TCH!=
19  Nan:      =A:bby jus'side with the=
20            =mo::[:m, ]
21  Hyl:           [ekhh]
22  Hyl:      u-I wz so [mad et [that.]
23  Nan:                [ G o : [: : d].
24            (.)
25  Nan: -->  You- .tch! How c'n she say tha:t
26            (.)
27  Hyl:      't's easy.=She writes it out.=
28  Hyl:      =.hhhh[hhh [(bak(hh)ay)hhh:hinh
29  Nan:           [Oh: [(bo:y)
30  Hyl:      hinh
31            (0.2)
32  Nan:      No: I think that's ah[:ful.]
```

After Hyla summarizes Abby's advice (lines 13–15), completing her story, Nancy displays her understanding of and alignment with the story in two ways: first, by displaying a stance in sympathy with the girl in the story: "Oh:::-::::." (line 16), then by providing an upshot of the advice, "A:bby jus'side with the mo:::m," (lines 19–20). As she hears Hyla begin to display a more emphatic negative stance (line 22), Nancy also upgrades her stance with "G o ::: d." (line 23). She subsequently asks a wh-question that challenges Abby's advice, "How c'n she say tha:t" (line 25), further aligning with Hyla's stance. As Clayman (2002:5) says, "At one level, this question seeks an explanation for Abby's action. At the same time, however, it seems to imply rather strongly that there is no acceptable explanation for Abby's conduct, and hence that the question is not readily answerable." This question is thus similar to the wh- RPQs discussed earlier. Hyla's response, "'t's easy.=She writes it out." (line 27), comes off as a joke because it treats this question as a "real", information-seeking question rather than as an RPQ challenge. In fact, this kind of question is only answerable as a joke.

So far we have seen that wh-questions can be used to as challenges to both co-present parties and non-present parties. When used to challenge accusations made by co-present parties, the questions ask the accuser to provide support for the accusation, and, at the same time, imply that no support can be found and that the accusation is thus untenable. In the analysis of wh-question challenges to non-present parties, we saw how these questions can be used to challenge reported actions as well as prior talk. We will now turn to a discussion of a specific type of challenge: a complaint.

3.4 Wh-questions used as complaints

The question words *how come* and *why* are especially suited for producing complaints when they are heard as RPQs. They challenge the appropriateness of an action. Similar to *how can* (+ *pronoun*), *how come* and *why* ask for an account of a particular action, but at the same time, suggest that there is no adequate account available.

3.4.1 *How come*

Both *how come* and *why* can be used to complain about unfair treatment by setting up a contrast that displays this unfairness. In the following excerpt, also discussed in Clayman (2002), Joan is telling Linda about problems she has had ordering from a particular company. She uses a *how come* RPQ (lines 15–17) to contrast her friend Chleo's success with her own problems getting her order filled.

```
(25)   [Linda and Joan 1: 38]
       01 Joa:      =.hhhhhhhhhhh n-Well Chleo tol' me
       02                          thet she hed jist ordered those
       03                          item:s, en got thum last week.
       04                          hhhhhhhhmhh
       05 Lin:      Oh::,
       06 Joa:      .t.hhhh En nao:w, when she called
```

```
07                  th'company, (.) they don't have um.
08  Lin:            Oh::[:,
09  Joa:                [.t.hhhh (  )um really
10                  disgusted now I aftih tell those
11                  people thet- we don't (.) yih
12                  [know well they don't have'em yih
13  Lin:            [Yeah.
14  Joa:            gitcher money back b't yet .hhhhh
15        -->       How come Chleo got um yihknow en
16        -->       here I've been waiting fer two
17        -->       months.hh.khh
18  Lin:            Ye:ah.
19                  (.)
20  Lin:            Ri:ght.=
21  Joa:            =That's what rilly made me ma:d.=
```

Joan asks the RPQ in lines 15–17 in the environment of a complaint, having already described her disgust at not having the items she had tried to order (lines 9–12). In producing the RPQ, she uses contrastive stress on the two person references, "Chleo" and "I", to contrast the difference in treatment that she and Chleo have received by the retail company. She seems to be asking for an account for this unequal treatment, and at the same time, suggesting that there is no adequate account available. Linda treats this utterance as a complaint, rather than as an information-seeking question. She responds with "Ye:ah. (.) Ri:ght." (lines 18–20), agreeing with the assertion conveyed through the question, i.e., that there is no adequate account available. Joan subsequently refers to this issue of unfair treatment as her main complaint, i.e., "what rilly made me ma:d." (line 21).

3.4.2 *Why*

Why questions can also be used in similar ways to complain about unfair treatment. In the following excerpt, discussed by Schegloff (1984:33), a husband and wife are discussing arrangements for visiting another couple. Their 1 1/2-year-old daughter is playing on the floor beside them. The wife uses a *why* RPQ (line 1) to complain about the arrangements.

```
(26)
    01  W:  -->  Why is it that we have to go there.
    02  H:       Because she ((head-motioning to
    03            daughter)) can go out more easily
    04            than their kids can.
```

As in the previous excerpt, the wife uses contrastive stress to display the unfairness of the proposed arrangements. But rather than explicitly contrasting the treatment she and her husband are receiving with that of the couple they are visiting, she uses contrastive stress on "we" and "there" to highlight the inconvenience that she and her husband face, leaving her preferred alternative, that "*they* have to come *here*", inexplicit. Heard as an RPQ, "Why is it that we have to go there.", implies that there is no adequate reason why W and her husband should be the ones who are inconvenienced. By answering with a reason, "Because she can go out more easily than their kids can." (lines 2–4), H disagrees with the implication of W's RPQ, displaying lack of alignment with her complaint. The contrast that H sets up, by means of contrastive stress on "*she*" and "*their* kids", argues against the complaint of unfairness proposed by his wife.

Why RPQs can also be used as complaints where there are no claims of unfairness, as in the following example discussed by Yoon (in progress).[23] Two female roommates, native speakers of Korean living in the U.S., are preparing dinner for friends. The elder, Young, looks into the stew pot, begins adding more vegetables, and then complains about the amount.

(27) **Yoon: Dinner Talk**

```
01 Young:      [te ] manhi nuh-ci:
               more a.lot put-COM
               [((looking at stew on table))
               ((You)) should've put mo:re
               ((vegetables into the stew))
02       -->   way yo -mankhum ne-ss-tay:¿
         -->   why this -as.much.as put-PST-Q
         -->   Why did ((you)) put so few:
03             (0.5)
04 Young:      ippu-m-- ippu[m    -ma]
               pretti-- prettiness-only
05 Jeong:                  [ pan--  ]
                           [Half--
06 Young:      [n kangc]ohay-ss -kwuna.
               emphasize -PST-I.found
               Pretti-- ((you)) were just
               emphasizing how pretty it
               looked right.
07 Jeong:      pan -ssik (.)
               half-each
08             itta (neh-ul)lakwu.
               later put-intending.to
               ((That's only)) half (.)
```

```
                        ((I)) intended to add
                        ((the rest)) later.
    09  Young:          a: kulay?
                        O:h is that so?
```

Young tells her roommate Jeong she should have added more vegetables to the stew, implying that the amount Jeong has prepared is insufficient (line 1). In this environment, where a recipient's action has already been characterized as problematic, a *why* question that asks for an account of that action (line 2) can further problematize it. According to Yoon (in progress), "*yo*", is a diminutive form. By stressing it, Young implies that the amount is *too* little. Young's *why* question can therefore be heard as an RPQ. Like the questions in Excerpts 25 and 26, it ostensibly asks for an account of an action, and at the same time, conveys that no adequate account exists. After Young provides a mock account (line 6) that is obviously inadequate, Jeong provides an account for why there are so few vegetables in the stew (line 8).

We have seen how a series of wh-questions can be used to refer to a prior utterance or to an action, challenging the grounds for that utterance or action. This is done by asking a question that the questioner implies is unanswerable. The questions in Excerpts 19–23 are ostensibly asking the recipient to support a prior accusation (by asking for an instance of the behavior of which the participant was accused), but at the same time implying that this support does not exist; there is thus no basis for the original claim. The *how* and *why* questions in Excerpts 24–27 perform a similar action. They ask for an account of an action, but at the same time imply that there is no adequate account available. The questions are able to accomplish this because, even though they are designed grammatically as questions, they are not used to ask for information but rather to convey the epistemic stance of the questioner.[24]

3.5 Wh-question challenges in institutional talk

We saw in Chapter 2 that yes/no RPQs can be used as challenges both in ordinary, mundane conversation and in different types of institutional talk, specifically broadcast news interviews and pedagogical interactions. Similarly, wh-RPQs can also be used as challenges in institutional talk. They can be used, as in ordinary conversation, to convey negative assertions that challenge grounds for a prior claim. However, even though RPQs can be used to accomplish the same action in institutional settings, the claims and challenges to those claims can also reflect institutional norms and roles and help to further institutionally specific goals or mandates (cf. Drew & Heritage 1992a; Maynard 1984). Institutional norms and roles can thus be enacted, and goals accomplished, by means of practices of talk that are not themselves institutionally specific.

I demonstrate this by explicating two excerpts with similar wh-question challenges in two different institutional settings. The first data excerpt was partially discussed in Chapter 2 as Excerpt 16. It is taken from a one-on-one conference between a writing teacher and an undergraduate second language student. They are meeting together to discuss how to revise a draft of the student's paper on Charles de Gaulle's leadership. A copy of the relevant portion of the student's paper is provided prior to the transcript of Excerpt 16.

```
(28)    TC/SD:7
        61  TC:       ok. ((reading)) "according to de
        62             Gaulle" ((she meant "Gardner"))
        63             ↓here's what you say "according
        64             to de Gaulle leaders are char-
        65             categorized as direct indirect
        66             (0.2) ordinary innovative (0.8)
        67             or: visionary."↓
        68             (1.5) ((TC eyegaze on text;
        69             bent over text))
        70             why did you: talk about that.
        71             (0.8) ((TC moves paper toward SD;
        72             straightens body;
        73             eyegaze still on text))
        74  SD:       uh s- [cause (0.8) d- this one of
        75                   [((TC looks up briefly at
        76             SD, then down at text))
        77             the sources that we (.) read in
        78             cla[ss.
        79  TC:          [um [hum?
        80  SD:              [so I jus wanted ta include
        81             that. as uh: information.
        82             (0.5) ((TC eyegaze on SD))
        83  TC:       Is it relevant?
        84             *to what you're saying?
        85             (0.8)* ((*SD looks down))
        86  SD:       No it's just background. heh h
        87  TC:       It's background?=
        88  SD:       =yeah.=
        89  TC:  -->  ok how's it background.=because I-
        90             like .h most people wouldn't
        91             know[:
```

```
92  SD:         [((sniff))
93  TC:         maybe what he meant by direct
94              indirect ordinary innovative or
95              visionary.
96  SD:         (yeah.)/(well) o̲k,
97              (1.5) ((SD nods))
```

As discussed in Chapter 2, there are two issues being worked through here. One is that SD has introduced many leadership terms from Gardner (1996): "direct, indirect, ordinary, innovative, and visionary," most of which are not relevant to his essay on de Gaulle. Only the first, *direct* leadership, is relevant. The second issue is one of *recipient design* (Sacks et al. 1974): SD has introduced the terms without defining them, as if writing for the teacher or other members of his class. When TC asks the question, "Is it relevant? to what you're saying?" (lines 83–84), she is implying that these categories are not relevant to what SD had earlier agreed he was focusing on in his paper, and therefore should be eliminated. This type of yes/no RPQ will be discussed in Chapter 4.

Although SD agrees with the teacher's criticism that what he has written is not relevant to what he is saying about de Gaulle, he does not seem to see or agree with the implication that it should be eliminated. He answers with an aligned "no" but then adds an utterance that makes his agreement somewhat equivocal: "it's just background. heh h" (line 86). Although the word *just* displays agreement with TC's implied criticism, i.e., it's *just* background, not relevant to his main thesis, SD seems to be justifying including it as background.

However, because SD has introduced these terms without providing any explanation for the reader, they would not provide the readers with background to help them understand the remainder of the text. TC chooses to deal with this issue before returning to the issue of relevance. She challenges SD's assertion with another question done as a next turn repair initiation (line 87):

```
86  SD:  No it's just background. heh h
87  TC:  It's background?=
```

As discussed in Chapter 2, TC's question, "It's background?", is used as a pre-disagreement, taking a form common to pre-disagreements (Schegloff 1997a; Schegloff et al. 1977), i.e., a partial repetition of the prior utterance with question intonation. Pre-disagreements are designed to provide an opportunity for a backdown, which would eliminate the necessity for a full disagreement. This pre-disagreement, however, does not get a backdown. There is no evidence, in fact, that SD sees this as a pre-disagreement. He treats this partial repetition as a simple request for confirmation of what he has just said, providing a confirmation in a preferred manner:

```
87 TC:    It's background?=
88 SD:    =yeah.=
```

TC's position, that this portion of SD's text is irrelevant and needs to be eliminated, is threatened by SD's assertion that it's background (and therefore has a place in this paper). When TC questions this assertion with a predisagreement, and SD maintains his position rather than backing down, TC continues by disagreeing with, or challenging SD's assertion that the problematic portion of text can be characterized as background. She does this using a wh-question (line 89) similar to those used by Shelley to challenge Debbie's accusations:

```
89 TC:  -->  ok how's it background.=because I-
90              like .h most people wouldn't
91              know[:
92 SD:              [((sniff))
93 TC:          maybe what he meant by direct
94              indirect ordinary innovative or
95              visionary.
96 SD:          (yeah.)/(well) ok,
97              (1.5) ((SD nods))
```

The utterance, "ok how's it background." (line 89), shares many similarities with Shelley's "when" questions in Excerpts 19–22 and Mark's "where" question in Excerpt 23.[25] It is built as a grammatically affirmative wh-question (it contains no negative markers such as "not" or "never"). It occurs in the environment of a disagreement, here, in the third turn after a pre-disagreement that did not engender a backdown. And it conveys a negative assertion that challenges the grounds for a prior claim, suggesting that there is no basis for that claim. In this excerpt, the wh-question takes the form of asking for an account for the previous assertion, "it's just background." (line 86), thereby making it accountable, i.e., "On what grounds do you assert that it's background?" It does this by repeating elements of the assertion and adding a wh-question word that ordinarily asks for an account. But, like the wh-questions used by Shelley to challenge Debbie's accusations, the utterance is not actually asking for an account; it seems rather to be challenging the student's assertion by contradicting it, saying, in effect, "It's not background", implying that an account for that claim is not available.

Also, like Shelley in Excerpt 20, the teacher designs the remainder of the turn in a way that does not invite an answer to the *how* question, showing that this question is meant to be understood as an assertion rather than an information-seeking question. The *how* question is followed immediately, without a beat of silence, by an increment-like continuation: "=because I- like .h most people wouldn't know: maybe what he meant by direct indirect ordinary innovative or visionary." (lines 89–95). In this addition the teacher gives her own account for the position she just indirectly asserted, i.e., that merely listing leadership types is not providing the readers with background (to understand the rest of the essay) because most people would not know what Gardner meant by these terms. This is very similar to MacNeil's yes/no RPQ in Excerpt 10, Chapter 2: "will he really,=because some people are already calling him irrelevant, or an american puppet, or (.)". Although this is not a canonical *increment* because it does not add a grammatically compatible clause to the first question, it acts like an increment semantically when the *how* question is interpreted as a negative assertion. The *because* clause fits both semantically and grammatically, not with the *how* question, but with its implied negative assertion, i.e., "It's not background because most people wouldn't know maybe what he meant by direct indirect ordinary innovative or visionary."

SD's response to TC's turn also displays an orientation to the turn as asserting a claim rather than asking for information. SD's response, "(yeah.)/(well) ok,", along with his nod (lines 96–97), are not responses to a *how* information-seeking question. If what SD said was "yeah." (one of the two alternate hearings), he would be displaying agreement with TC's argument. The "ok," displays acceptance of the argument. A "well ok," would be a somewhat hesitant acceptance. That SD understands and accepts TC's argument is demonstrated a few minutes later when SD collaboratively completes TC's utterance (Lerner 1987, 1989, 1991, 1996) as TC begins to give explicit advice on incorporating background information:

(29) TC/SD:12

```
192 TC:      That's fine ta do it that way.=
193          um: (0.5) .h but when yer- (2.8)
194          when yer um: (1.0) mentioning
195          this background information?=like
196          you called it background
197          in[formation, .hh ya
198 SD:        [yeah,
199 TC:      know: (.) [try ta think about- ]
200 SD: -->            [I have ta explain   ]
201     -->  (it)/(them)?
```

SD collaboratively completes TC's "when" clause, "when yer- (2.8) when yer um: (1.0) mentioning this background information?" with "I have ta explain (it)/(them)?" This completion demonstrates SD's understanding of TC's earlier utterance, i.e., that labels from the readings cannot be considered background for the reader if the reader does not understand what the terms mean. It may also demonstrate a changed understanding of who the audience is for this paper.

In the above excerpt, an utterance built as a grammatically affirmative wh-question was used by a teacher, not to ask for information, but to challenge a student's prior claim in a way that resembles its use in ordinary conversation. In both settings, wh-questions were used in the environment of a disagreement. The questions conveyed negative assertions that challenged the grounds for prior assertions which threatened the questioner's position. However, in the institutional setting, the challenge was used to further an institutionally specific goal (cf. Drew & Heritage 1992a), to correct a student's understanding of how to incorporate background reading in an academic essay. As such, this challenge also displays the teacher's role as that of expert on norms of American academic discourse, one whose job is to assist novice writers to revise their drafts according to these norms. The wh-question challenge, and the grounds given for it, also reflect a specific norm for many college writing classes for international students, i.e., that student essays need to be written for an abstract audience who is not familiar with the class readings.

We can see a similar orientation to pedagogical roles and goals with the yes/no RPQs discussed in Excerpts 16 and 17. The discussion of this same interaction in Excerpt 16 focused on the teacher's use of a pre-disagreement, "It's background?" to challenge the student's claim that his list of leadership types can provide the reader with background (necessary to understand the rest of his essay). In Excerpt 17, the teacher used a yes/no RPQ, "daughters:" to question a student's answer and elicit a self-correction.

In the following excerpt from a broadcast news interview,[26] the earlier portion of which is discussed in Heritage (2002b), and in Chapter 2, a turn design that is almost identical to TC's wh-question RPQ is used by an interviewee, then president Clinton, for a similar purpose, i.e., to challenge an assertion made in a prior turn. This prior assertion, like those in Excerpts 19–23, is done as an accusation, and the wh-question is used to challenge that accusation by challenging the grounds on which it is based. However, as in Excerpt 28, the wh-question is used in the context of accomplishing institutionally-specific goals, and it similarly helps to formulate and display institutional roles. The excerpt begins with the interviewer's accusation:

(30) Clinton Press Conference
```
01  IR:    W'l Mister President in your zea:l
02         (.) for funds during the last
03         campaign .hh didn't you put the
04         Vice President (.) an' Maggie and
05         all the others in your (0.4)
06         administration top side .hh in a
07         very vulnerable position, hh
08         (0.5)
09  IE:    I disagree with that,=h (0.8) u-
10    -->  How are we vulnerable because .hh
11         only vulnerable if you think it is
12         inherently ba:d ta raise funds..hh
13         and you believe that these
14         transactions are between people
15         who are .hh almost craven.=I mean
16         (I do- wa-) that's how uh- I I (.)
17         I don't agree with that. I .h
```

The interviewer's question is one of a set of questions discussed in Heritage (2002a) which are used by hostile interviewers as challenges. Though grammatically negative, incorporating phrases such as *isn't it* or *don't you*, these questions are heard by interviewees as affirmative assertions, displaying the epistemic stance of the interviewer. Clinton's response, "I disagree with that," shows that he views the interviewer as having made an assertion which can be disagreed with, i.e., "you put the Vice President an' Maggie and all the others in your administration top side in a very vulnerable position."

After his explicit statement of disagreement, Clinton goes on to specify what it is he disagrees with. The utterance, "How are we vulnerable ..." (line 10), like the teacher's "ok how's it background." (Excerpt 28), takes the form of asking for an account of the previous assertion embedded in the interviewer's question, thereby making that assertion accountable. But, like the teacher's question, it is not actually asking for an account; it seems rather to be challenging the interviewer's assertion by implying that an account for this assertion is not available, i.e., "We're not vulnerable." Clinton then goes on to give an account that justifies his claim, i.e., that they would only be vulnerable if one had an exaggeratedly negative view of fundraising. In Excerpt 30, as in Excerpt 28, the *how* question is not meant to be answered; it is the interviewer's, not the interviewee's, role to ask questions. As in Excerpt 28, the design of the turn following the question displays that it is not asking for information. The *how* question is immediately followed by an increment-like addition which fits, grammatically and semantically, with the negative assertion "we are not vulnerable", providing an account to justify this assertion.[27]

Although the turn design and action it is doing are almost identical to TC's turn in Excerpt 28, the wh-question in Excerpt 30 is used in a different institutional context reflecting a different set of institutional norms and roles. According to Heritage (2002a), broadcast news interviewers operate under two competing norms. On the one hand, they are expected to take an impartial, objective, "neutralistic" stance toward interviewees (Clayman 1988; Heritage & Greatbatch 1991); on the other hand, they ascribe to a "norm of adversarialness" which challenges their interviewees. Both of these norms are exemplified in the interviewer's question to Clinton. The "norm of adversarialness" is oriented to by the challenge implied in the negatively-formatted RPQ, a challenge that Clinton does some work to defend himself against. Yet the question format enables the interviewer to sustain the fiction that she is merely asking a question, not offering an opinion. Clinton, in his role of interviewee, exposes this fiction by both explicitly disagreeing with the accusation implied by the question, and by challenging the grounds for this accusation, using a wh-question challenge. In contrast to the teacher's use of a wh-question challenge for pedagogical purposes, here, Clinton uses an almost identical wh-question challenge to defend himself against a hostile interviewer. Similarly, yes/no RPQs were used by the teachers in Excerpts 16 and 17 to initiate error correction, but by the interviewers in Excerpts 5–7 and 10 to challenge interviewees and, at the same time, maintain the fiction that they are merely asking questions. Institutional roles can thus be enacted, and goals accomplished, by means of practices of talk that are not institutionally specific.

3.6 Misunderstanding the sequential implicativeness of wh-questions

Two instances of misunderstanding discussed in Schegloff (1987b) provide examples of recipients understanding wh-questions as negative assertions, even when they were meant as ordinary information-seeking questions. Both of these instances therefore exemplify misunderstanding the "sequential implicativeness" (Schegloff 1987b) of the turns in question. In other words, the parties had different understandings about what action was being done in the turn in question, and, consequently, what that turn's sequential import was, i.e., what would be relevant as a next turn response. The first example is from a call to a suicide prevention center. The caller, G (Mr. Greenberg) is talking to a staff member (S):

(31) (SPC, 74)
```
01  G:   Well what did Miss Jevon say when
02       you spoke to her.
03  S:   She said she would be glad to talk
04       to you and she would be waiting for
05       your call.
06  G:   Boy, it was some wait. Everyone
07       else in that clinic has just been
08       wonderful to me. Both the diabetic
09       clinic and the psychiatric clinic.
10       It's just that woman.
11  S: --> Well, what are you going to do,
12       Mr. Greenberg.
13  G:   Well that's true. When you are a
14       charity patient, when you are a
15       beggar, you just can't do anything
16       about it, you just have to take
17       what's handed out to you, and-
18  S:   No, I mean about yourself. What
19       are you going to do for yourself.
20       You were wondering what to do for
21       yourself, you called me and told me
22       you were thinking about having
23       yourself admitted to a state
24       hospital ...
```

After Mr. Greenberg complains about another member of staff (lines 6–10), the staff member he has been talking to asks a wh-question, "well, what are you going to do, Mr. Greenberg." (lines 11–12). This question, as is shown in the repair in lines 18–24, was meant as a request for information about Mr. Greenberg's plans. However, Mr. Greenberg, in his response (lines 13–17), displays a different understanding of the question. He first agrees with it, showing that he has heard the questioner to be making an assertion, rather than asking for information: "Well that's true." (line 13). Mr. Greenberg then makes explicit his understanding of what he heard that assertion to be: "When you are a charity patient, when you are a beggar, *you just can't do anything about it*" (lines 13–16). In other words, he has heard "What are you going to do" as "There's nothing you can do", implying that he has no options but to take what he is given, because of his status as a charity patient.

The following example, from a radio call-in show, contains a similar misunderstanding. B has called to discuss a problem she has.

(32) (BC, Beige, 14)
```
01  B:        ... but- hh lately? I have fears
02            a' driving over a bridge.
03            ((silence))
04  B:        A:nd uh seems I uh- I just can't uh
05            (sit)- if I hevuh haftuh cross a
06            bridge I jus', don't (go an'
07            make- uh- do the) trip at all.
08  A: -->    Whaddyuh afraid of.
09  B:        I dun'kno:w, see uh
10  A:        Well I mean waitam'n.
11            What kind of fear is it.
12            'R you afraid yer gunnuh
13            drive off the e:dge?
14            'R you afraid thet uh yer gunnuh
15            get hit while yer on it?
16            [What.
17  B:        [Off the edge 'r sumthin.
```

In this example, A's "Whaddyuh afraid of." (line 8) was intended as a request for information, as seen in A's repair (lines 10–15). The fact that A felt it necessary to do a repair at this point shows that A hears B's response in line 9 as displaying a different understanding of "Whaddyuh afraid of." This alternate response, according to Schegloff (1987b), implies that "there's nothing to be afraid of", and B's response, I dun' kno:w, (line 9), displays an agreement with this stance.

In both of the above examples, even though the questioners' "third position repairs" (Schegloff 1987b, 1992) display that they were merely asking for information, the recipients display a hearing of the wh-question turns as negative assertions, used to challenge a prior utterance. Rather than challenging the grounds for a prior assertion as do the questions in Excerpts 19–23, 28, and 30, these questions, when heard as challenges, challenge the grounds for an action done or trouble expressed in the prior turn. In Excerpt 31, the staff member's question, "Well, what are you going to do, Mr. Greenberg.", when heard as a challenge, challenges his right to complain. Similarly, the talk show host's question, "Whaddyuh afraid of.", if heard as a challenge, challenges the caller's right to be afraid. Each of these are heard as challenges by hearing the wh-question, not as asking for information, but as conveying a negative assertion, i.e., "There's nothing you can do"; "There's nothing to be afraid of."

3.7 Summary of analysis

So far I have discussed a type of wh-question used as a challenge to a prior utterance or an action. The questions occur in environments of already-established disagreements, challenges, or complaints. When they challenge prior utterances, the questions refer back to the utterance they are challenging through substitution, by incorporating elements of the prior utterance into their design, or by adjacent positioning after the targeted utterance. Like yes/no RPQs, these wh-questions are able to do challenging because, rather than asking for new information, they are used to convey a strong epistemic stance of the questioner, specifically a negative assertion. The negative assertions claim that there is no basis for claims, actions, or feelings expressed through the utterances they challenge. Also like yes/no RPQs, the wh-questions can be accompanied by accounts that give the grounds for the challenge. The accounts can be done as increment-like utterances, latched onto the wh-question, and fitted grammatically and semantically to the implied negative assertion, rather than to the question form of the utterance. By latching accounts or other utterances to the wh-questions, speakers can display that they are not inviting answers to the questions. This does not mean that recipients of wh-question challenges never answer them as questions. However, when responses are given, the responders orient to the questions as doing challenging, e.g., by accepting the challenge (Excerpt 28), agreeing with it (Excerpt 25), backing down from the prior claim (Excerpt 22), eventually aligning with the challenger (Excerpt 23), or challenging the appropriateness of the challenge (Excerpts 26–27).

3.8 Canonical wh-question challenges

Earlier I suggested that *how can (+ pronoun)* challenges may be especially vulnerable to being heard as canonical challenges. Here I discuss two other practices that can be considered canonical challenges, for different reasons. Both practices differ slightly from the wh- RPQ challenges already discussed.

3.8.1 *What do you mean (+ X)*

The wh-question challenges described above, especially those with a "how… because…" construction, show similarities to a practice for challenging discussed by (Schegloff 1997a): "What do you mean + X", where "X" is an additional component which provides the grounds for the challenge, as in the following examples:

(33) **NB**
```
01  Agn:     W'l that's not therapeutic Clara,
02           really, It says on the (0.4)-
03           thing, uh-theh-when yih- uh this
04           proxide is uh kind of a- (0.2)
05           .hhhhh
06  Cla: --> Whaddiyuh mean uh-th-uh doctors
07           use it,
08           (0.8)
09  Agn:     .hh W'l on the little jar it says
10           not therapeutic so,
```

(34) **Auto Discussion**
```
01  Cur:     He- he's about the only regular
02           <he's about the only good regular
03           out there 'z, keegan still go
04           out?
05  Mik:     Keegan's, out there he's, He run,
06           (0.5)
07  Mik:     E:[r he's uh::    ]=
08  Gar: -->   [Wuhyih mean my:,]
09       -->  My [brother in law's out there, ]
10  Mik:        =[doin real good this year'n ]
11              M'Gilton's doin real good
12              thi[s year,
13  Cur:          [M'Gilton still there?
```

In Excerpt 33, Clara is challenging her sister's claim that a salve is not therapeutic, on the grounds that the doctors use it (lines 6–7). Agnes responds to Clara's utterance as a challenge by giving an account for her prior claim in a dispreferred manner (lines 9–10), displaying its status as a disagreement. The turn itself is delayed with a .8 second silence (line 8), and the account is further delayed within its turn by an in-breath and "w'l". In Excerpt 34, Gary is challenging Curt's claim that Al, the "he" in line 1, is the only good regular at the automobile races, on the grounds that his brother-in-law also races (lines 8–9). Gary's challenge is done in overlap with Mike's turn (lines 7 and 10) and is ignored by both Mike and Curt.

The format, "what do you mean" + grounds for the challenge, parallels the "How… because…" format seen in Excerpts 29 and 31. Both practices give the challenge in the form of a wh-question followed immediately by the grounds for the challenge. Like the challenges in Excerpts 19–21, the "what do you mean" challenges in Excerpts 33 and 34 do not refer anaphorically back to the turn they are challenging through substitution or by incorporating elements of the targeted turn in their design. They do so by adjacency, i.e., by being located in the very next turn, they target the utterance in the prior turn. However, there is evidence that speakers do, at times, incorporate elements of the targeted turn in "what do you mean" challenges as did speakers in Excerpts 23, 28, and 30. In the following excerpt, discussed earlier as Excerpt 8, Marsha, in an argument with her son Joseph, uses a "what do you mean + X" challenge; however, "X" is not an account for the challenge but a partial repetition (with changes for deictic reference) of the turn she is challenging:

(35) **Marcia & Joseph**

```
09 Mar:     I don't think I'm harming
10          anybu:ddy,
11          (0.3)
12 Jos:     AH WASN HARMING ANYBUDDY EITHER.
13          (0.5)
14 Mar: --> Waddiyou mean you weren't harming
15          anyb[uddy
16 Jos:         [BY GOINGDA SCHOO:L WITH A
17          BROKEN COLLARBONE THAT GAVE YOU
18          THE PUNISHMENT 'N THE FIRS(T)
19          PLA[CE,
20 Mar:        [( )ING) ANYBU:DDY,
21          (0.9)
22 Jos:     I WAS HARMING YOU,
23          (1.2)
24 Mar:     ↑YE:AH:: YOU HAVEN'T LEARNED T'
25          GET ALO:NG HERE AT A:LL.=
```

As discussed earlier, Marsha's utterance in lines 14–15 is not a request for clarification, nor is it treated as such by Joseph, even though "what do you mean + partial repeat of a prior turn" can also be used simply as a repair initiator, asking a "real" question, and not as a challenge. This is exemplified in the following excerpt, discussed in (Schegloff 1997a). Freda and Rubin have just complimented Kathy on an item that she has woven.

(36) **KC-4, 16**

```
05 Kat:     It wove itself once it was set
06          up.=
07 Fre:     =Its woo:l?
08 Kat:     It's wool.
09          (0.8)
```

```
10  Rub:  -->  Whaddyou mean it wove itself once
11             it w's set up.=
12             =[What d's that] mean.=
13  Kat:       =[Oh i-        ]
14  Kat:       =Well I mean it's ve:ry simple,
```

Here Rubin's *what do you mean* + repetition of the trouble source turn (lines 10–11) is correctly taken to be a repair initiation. In fact, he seems to be taking steps to ensure that it is heard as a repair initiation rather than a challenge: he follows this TCU immediately with a second TCU (line 12) that disambiguates the first.

One important difference between the *what do you mean* + repetition of a prior turn in Excerpts 35 and 36 is the environment of ongoing argument/disagreement already in progress in Excerpt 35 which, as I discussed earlier in the analysis of Excerpt 8, contributes to the turn's being heard as a challenge, and not a repair initiator.

What do you mean challenges are thus similar in many respects to the wh-question challenges that I have described in Excerpts 19–30. They are designed as wh-questions that, in other sequential contexts, could be used as "real" information-seeking questions. They can incorporate elements of the turn they are challenging, as well as accounts for the challenge, in their design. However, they differ in one respect from the wh-question challenges in Excerpts 19–30. Although they do convey disagreement with a prior assertion, they do not generally do this by conveying the corresponding negative assertion.[28] It may be that the *what do you mean* format has become such a canonical format for a challenge in certain sequential positions that it does not depend for its interpretation on an implied negative assertion.

3.8.2 *Who cares*

Another canonical challenge, *who cares*, is exemplified in the next excerpt taken from an American middle-class family dinner with two adopted boys, Sam and John, both age 12.[29] As the excerpt begins, there has just been some teasing between Dad and John, and Dad is laughing at a comeback from John. Mom introduces a new topic: making arrangements for the next morning. During the course of this talk, John makes a grammar error (line 26), which is addressed by the other family members (lines 30, 32–33). John challenges this focus on his grammar with a wh-question: "OH WHO CA:RES." (line 35).

(37)   **Scarborough: Family Dinner**

```
01 Dad:     [ha ha ha ha    ]
02 Mom:     [Ok. To mo rro:w.] Tomorrow.
03 Dad:     Yes,
04 Mom:     um (.) morning. .hhh would you
05          like me to take Sam to school?=
06 Dad:     =no.=(>I want you to<)/(jist)
07          take John.
08          (0.8)
09 Joh:     [(so did I)]
10 Mom:     [(I (    )] can't take John tomorrow,
11 Dad:     Why,
12 Mom:     because I have to sub at nine.
13 Dad:     Ok, I guess uh: (1.5) yeah, you
14          can take Sam if you want,
15 Mom:     ok.
16 Joh:     He just doesn't like me because I
17          like him to take the most direct
18          .hhh a:nd
19          (1.2)
20 Mom:     because you <like to be driving
21          just like> channeling through him
22          and he li- has his own mind
23          and likes to choose [where he=
24 Dad:                         [Yeah]
25 Mom:     =drives,
26 Joh:     I just like to take the *directest
27          route so we can get there on
28          ti:me,*= ((In singsong voice from
29          * to *))
30 Mom:     =directest?
31 Joh:     [directest.]
32 Sam:     [direct]
33 Dad:     mo[st direct.        ]
34 Mom:       [(that's not ( )]
35 Joh: --> OH WHO CA:RES.
36          (1.0)
37 Sam:     We're not in school right [now
38 Dad:                               [Well:,
39          <when you're taking the ay cee tee
40          ((i.e., ACT)). (0.2) the scor:es
41          of the test will care,> >when
42          you're taking< the es es ay tee
43          ((i.e. SSAT)) (.) <the scores of
44          the test [will care,>
```

```
45  Joh:            [um I don't write that,
46  Sam:            And that's usually a machine,
47  Mom:            Anyway, (1.8) I'm afraid if I take
48                  ↑him: (0.8) unless I can leave him
49                  there,
```

When Mom offers to take Sam to school (lines 4–5), Dad makes it clear that he wants her to take John instead (lines 6–7). After Mom explains why she can't take John (lines 10, 12), John provides an account for why Dad doesn't like to take him to school (lines 16–18). During the course of this account, he uses the correct superlative form of *direct*, i.e., "most direct". When Mom counters with an account that is more flattering to Dad and less flattering to John (line 20–23, 25) and Dad agrees with Mom's account (line 24), John reissues his former account: "I just like to take the *directest route so we can get there on ti:me,*" (lines 26–28), with the starred portion said in a sing-song voice. Mom initiates repair on the incorrect grammar by repeating it with upward intonation, as a prompt for John to self-correct, as in Excerpts 13–14 and 16–17. Rather than correcting the adjective to the form used in line 17, John repeats the error, possibly in defiance (line 31), at the same time that Sam, his brother, provides a correction (line 32). When Dad also follows with an explicit correction (line 33) and Mom, with a possible sanction (line 34), John yells "OH WHO CA:RES." (line 35). Unlike the *what do you mean* challenges, *who cares* does seem to convey a reversed polarity assertion, i.e., no one, including (or especially) myself, cares; this is not important. Sam aligns with his brother by providing an account for the assertion conveyed by this challenge: "We're not in school right now" (line 37). Dad, however, displays his disagreement with John's implied assertion by answering John's challenge as if it were a real question, listing two important tests that "will care" about John's grammar (lines 38–44). Dad's response is done in a slow, measured way that orients to the defiance in John's challenge.

Although the *who cares* challenge does seem to convey a reversed polarity assertion like the RPQs discussed above, it does not seem to be used in its free-standing form as a real, information-seeking question. As such, it can be considered a canonical form of challenge.

3.9 Interpretation of wh-question RPQs

Earlier we saw that yes/no RPQs may be understood as RPQs when they were asked from a position of epistemic strength. This claim may help explain how certain wh-questions are interpreted as conveying negative assertions rather than as information-seeking questions. The wh-questions discussed in Excerpts 19–23, 28, and 30 are all asked about subjects over which the questioner has greater claim to knowledge, either because the questions concern events which the questioners themselves have experienced, or because of the questioner has the role of expert in this domain, as does the teacher in the writing conference. When wh-questions are asked about subjects in the questioner's knowledge domain, and the questions are clearly not being used to test the recipient's knowledge, the questions may therefore be more likely to be interpreted as negative assertions used to do challenges.

The sequential environment in which these questions are asked, however, may provide an even greater clue to their interpretation. One of the features of wh-question challenges in Excerpts 19–30 is their occurrence in an already ongoing context of disagreement, challenge, complaint, and the like. An interpretation of a wh-question as a challenge would be especially likely in environments of disagreement, for example, after an accusation or after the questioner's position is threatened. In this environment, a challenge would be a relevant next action to perform. The sequential environment also helps explain why the recipients of wh-questions in Excerpts 31 and 32 misheard them as challenges, even though these questions were not asked about events to which the questioners, themselves, have primary access, as were the questions in Excerpts 19–23, 28, and 30.[30] In Excerpt 31 Mr. Greenberg had just criticized a staff member at the institution he was calling, and he heard the wh-question as a perhaps somewhat defensive challenge to his right to complain. In Excerpt 32, the caller, who had just described an irrational fear, heard the talk show host's wh-question as a challenge to the caller's right to be afraid. The recipients of these questions hear, in each case, a reversed polarity assertion doing a challenge as a sequentially appropriate next response. It thus becomes clear that, in the case of wh-question challenges, the form of the question by itself, apart from its context, does not determine its force. Neither does Bolinger's (1957) cognitive explanation sufficiently account for the interpretation of wh-questions as reversed polarity assertions, although parties to talk in interaction do seem to take into account the knowledge base of the questioner in determining how the question is to be understood. It is the interactional environment, specifically the orientation to a sequentially appropriate response, that is most important in interpreting the questions as reversed polarity assertions challenging a prior utterance.

CHAPTER 4

Yes/no reversed polarity questions used in pedagogically specific practices

1 Introduction

In the previous two chapters, we saw how RPQs can be used as challenges in a variety of settings. Those used in institutional settings orient to institutional roles and norms and can help accomplish institutional goals, even though their design and the actions they accomplish are similar, both in and outside of the specific institutional settings. Much of the conversation analytic work on talk in institutional settings, however, focuses on institutionally specific practices which help define talk in these particular settings (cf. Drew & Heritage 1992a). In this and the following chapter we will similarly investigate how RPQs are adapted for use in pedagogically specific ways. We will see how the RPQ turns themselves, and/or the sequences of action in which the RPQs are used, can be designed in different ways to accomplish certain pedagogically specific goals, and how special inferential frameworks (Drew & Heritage 1992a; Levinson 1979) may be used in interpreting the actions that these RPQs accomplish. The RPQ sequences discussed here and in Chapter 5 are therefore practices of pedagogical talk, rather than ordinary conversational practices which happen to be used in a pedagogical setting.

The RPQs analyzed in this chapter are used by teachers in one-on-one second language writing conferences. The writing conferences are held as part of a writing course for international and immigrant students enrolled at a large research university. The course functions as a bridge to freshman composition for undergraduates and fulfills an ESL (English as a Second Language) requirement for graduate students. Teachers of this course, experienced instructors and graduate teaching assistants, see their role as that of socializing students into the norms and practices of American academic written discourse. Among the resources that the teachers use to accomplish this goal are affirmative yes/no RPQs. They are used by teachers to help students diagnose problems in two different types of sequences and in different sequential environments in the two sequences. These two different environments create different preferences for a second pair part, or response, to the RPQ.

The first environment involves the use of yes/no RPQs in sequences focusing on enabling the student to find problems with content and organization, thereby ensuring that the student is able to solve these problems in a revision. In these sequences, both teachers and students display an orientation to *no* or its equivalent as a preferred answer. The second environment involves the use of yes/no RPQs in sequences where teachers are assisting students to self-correct grammar errors. In these sequences, a course of action has already been implemented: eliciting a knowledge display from the student. The RPQs are used as hints when students display problems giving a correct answer. The RPQs in this environment do not prefer an aligning *no* as an answer, but the action which an implied *no* answer makes relevant: a correct answer to the original question.

2 RPQs used as criticisms of student text

2.1 Introduction

RPQ sequences used to enable students to find and solve problems with content and organization are common in these writing conferences, occurring at least once and more often several times in most of the conferences I investigated. Like the grammatically affirmative yes/no RPQs described in Chapter 2, these questions convey a negative assertion. However, they are not used to challenge a prior utterance. In the sequential context in which they are used, they show what is problematic about a portion of student text and, in the process, point to a possible solution (although as I will show, the solution may not always be clear to the student). The teachers' goal is to ensure that the student is able to solve these problems in a later revision. Both teachers and students display an orientation to *no* or its equivalent as a preferred answer. *No* is the preferred answer because it aligns with the negative assertion conveyed by the RPQ. I also show that, as with RPQ challenges, the interpretation of these questions as negative assertions, rather than as "real," information-seeking questions, is based on the students' interpretation of the course of action in which the questions are embedded, and on the displayed knowledge state of the questioner, the teacher.

In this section I first discuss examples of RPQs with aligning responses, then an RPQ sequence where the student disagrees with the teacher. I follow these examples with an explication of a series of RPQ sequences from the same conference, showing the process through which a student comes to an understanding of a pedagogical point. Finally, I discuss the design of these RPQ sequences and show how they are understood by students to be doing criticism of their text.

2.2 RPQ with aligning response

In the conference from which the following excerpt is taken, the student and teacher are working on a draft of a paper on *Bystander Apathy*. The student, ST, is arguing that a proposed "Good Samaritan law" will not be effective in encouraging bystanders to get involved when witnessing an accident or a crime, as this law could not be enforced.

The interaction from which Excerpt 38 is taken begins halfway through the conference. The teacher, TJ, has just taken ST through a demonstration of two strategies for self-correcting verb tense and other language errors which, he says, will help improve ST's language and organization grades. TJ now focuses on the third component of the grade: content. In the following portion of transcript, TJ suggests that ST can improve the content of his paper by answering a comment, "So?" that he had written in two different places in the margin of ST's paper. He then checks to see if ST understands the meaning of the comment:

(38) TJ/ST
```
01 TJ:  now the content basically comes
02      fro:m (.) you.=an your head. .h an
03      the only way (.) that you can
04      improve the content is
05      [ta answer my questions when I say so. (2.0)]
06      [((TJ points to text, first page,
07      [then turns pages and points to
08      [ text again))
09      ya know what I mean by so?
10 ST:  no.
11      (0.2)
12 TJ:  ok.
```

After ST answers that he does not understand the "So?" comment, he briefly, and unsuccessfully, attempts to elicit an explanation of a different written comment (this portion of the transcript is omitted). TJ, however, as shown in the following portion of transcript, continues to pursue his earlier agenda. He begins an explication of the written comment "So?" by covering the top portion of ST's first paragraph with his hand, isolating the last sentence of that paragraph, the canonical place for a thesis statement in a student essay. TJ directs ST's attention visually to that sentence and reads it aloud. He then begins explaining the comment, using a series of questions, two of which are yes/no RPQs (lines 51 and 85).

```
33  TJ:   ok.
34        (0.8) ((TJ covers upper portion of
35        paper w/ palm))
36        'sus look at this.
37        (0.5) ((TJ eyegaze on text))
38        ((reading text)) "all these
39        situations (.) could have resulted
40        in better consequences, .h if any
41        of the bystanders had intervened
42        with the victims during their
43        struggle for help."
44        (2.0) ((TJ lateral headshake;
45        eyegaze on ST))
46        yeah?
47        (1.0) ((TJ & ST: mutual eyegaze))
48        so what.
49        *(2.0) / ((TJ eyegaze on ST; ST
50        eyegaze on paper from * to *))
51   -->  [is that what this paper's about?
52        [((TJ moves head to side as if to
53        meet ST's eyegaze))
54        (0.8)
55  ST:   no:,
56        (0.5)
57  TJ:   right.*
58        (0.2)
59        that's the problem.
60        (1.8) ((TJ & ST mutual eyegaze;
61        TJ smiles))
62        .h I don't understand what- (0.2)
63        yu- you give me these three uh:
64        very interesting: examples, .h an
65        you tie them together, .h
66        ((reading)) "all these situations
67        could've resulted in a better
68        consequences if anybody had gotten
69        involved."
70        (1.0) ((TJ & ST: eyegaze on text))
71        ok?
```

```
72              (0.5) ((TJ eyegaze on ST; ST
73              eyegaze on text; ST brief nod))
74              great.
75              (1.0) ((TJ eyegaze on ST;
76              ST eyegaze on text))
77              would've been different endings if
78              someone had gotten involved.
79      ST:     um hum
80              (0.8) ((TJ moves arms out in
81              shrugging gesture))
82      TJ:     so what.
83              (2.5) / ((TJ eyegaze on ST;
84              ST eyegaze on text))
85        -->  is that what the paper's about?
86      ST:     °no
87              (1.5) ((TJ eyegaze on ST;
88              ST eyegaze on text))
89      TJ:     somehow somewhere (0.2) in here,
90              *(2.0) ((TJ writing on text:
91              "What's this paper about?" from *
92              to *))
93              I need an answer to the question
94              what's this paper about.
95              (4.5)*
96              (3.0) ((TJ stops writing, leans
97              back, gazes at ST))
98              mkay?
99      ST:     um hum:
100             (1.0)
```

After reading the relevant portion of student text aloud, TJ asks a series of questions that explicate the meaning of the written comment "So?" which he has just told the student to take seriously in order to improve his content grade. The comment "So?" seems to be asking, "what is the relevance of this sentence to your paper?" After reading the student's sentence, the teacher first asks "yeah?" (line 46). Schegloff (1981) has demonstrated how tokens such as *uh huh* and *yeah*, which he calls *continuers*, are often used to pass an opportunity for a full turn at talk, demonstrating an understanding that another speaker intends to take an extended turn. Although this "yeah?" is not being used as a continuer here, TJ could be making use of this understanding to convey something like "surely you can't be done; this is part of a larger unit which I understand to not yet be finished," with the implication that "you should have finished it here and haven't." It says, or "does," in essence, "this isn't done; figure out what's missing and supply it."

TJ's "yeah?" is followed by a 1.0 second pause. ST is either interpreting the "yeah?" as a purely rhetorical question that is not meant to be answered at this point, or he does not have an answer for this question.

TJ next asks "so what." (line 48), a more direct explication of the written comment "So?" Both "so what." and "so?" are almost formulaic utterances that are used to challenge relevance. The question "so what." upgrades the amount of resources that the teacher is giving to the student to solve the problem of what is wrong with the sentence he has just read. If the student's sentence were relevant, there would be an answer to "so what." But because it is not relevant, at least according to TJ, there is no answer, and by asking this question TJ underscores that there is no answer. So this could also be considered a purely rhetorical question from TJ's point of view, a question to which he expects no answer. Indeed, the student treats it as such, giving no answer in the 2.0 seconds of silence following the question.

TJ then asks an RPQ, which again upgrades the amount of information that he has previously given ST about the problem: "is that what this paper's about?" (line 51). The pronoun "that" is used anaphorically to refer back to the portion of text that TJ had read and commented on. TJ seems to be using the RPQ in his explication of the written comment, "So?", to identify something problematic about the last sentence of the first paragraph, specifically, to question its relevance. The question seems to convey a negative observation: "that's not what this paper is about." In doing this, it shows what is problematic about this portion of text, and also suggests a solution: "this sentence *should* convey what the paper is about."

How does it do this? TJ has already read and commented on the paper. He is obviously not asking for information here. This is a *known-information* question (Mehan 1979a), one to which the teacher knows the answer, rather than a request for information. If the *known* answer to the question were *yes*, there would be nothing problematic about the student text under discussion here, and no reason to ask the question at this point. There is thus a sense that the teacher is conveying an implicit *no* answer to this question, the only answer which would further the course of problem-solving action begun in this sequence. By conveying a negative assertion about a portion of student text, RPQs can act as veiled criticisms of that text, showing that it is problematic and that it is problematic *for that reason*. This negative assertion conveyed by the RPQ shows why the portion of student text is problematic: it should say what the paper is about, but it does not.

ST gives an answer that aligns with the assertion conveyed through TJ's question: "no:," (line 55). ST's answer is slightly delayed, which may suggest that it is done as a dispreferred response. However, it is otherwise done as a preferred response: it is clear, straightforward, and unmitigated. The delay may have occurred because ST has to figure out if this is also a purely rhetorical question like the first two, or is meant to be answered.

ST's answer is followed, after a brief pause, by TJ's evaluation of the answer as correct: "right." (line 57), showing that the teacher saw *no* as the "correct" answer. TJ continues with a further utterance that displays what he was using the question to do: "that's the problem." (line 59). In other words, the problem is that the targeted text does not say what the paper is about.

TJ goes on to further explicate this problem (lines 62–78). He says that the examples ST provides are interesting and well-integrated, but he again questions their relevance by asking "so what." (line 82) and repeating the RPQ, "is that what the paper's about?" (line 85). This time ST's aligning "no" (line 86) is given immediately after the question in a clearly preferred manner. TJ ends this sequence by telling the student to provide, at this point in the paper, an answer to the question "What's this paper about?" (lines 89–94), writing the comment next to the "So?" at the end of the first paragraph.

In Excerpt 38 the teacher is using the two similar RPQs, by virtue of their ability to convey a negative assertion, to target what is problematic about a portion of the student's text and hint at what the solution might be to enable that student to self-correct. But because neither the RPQs nor the teacher's later suggested remedy make the solution explicit, there is room for student misinterpretation. TJ conveys in this excerpt that he does not see the relevance of the targeted sentence to the main argument of the paper. There is evidence that what TJ seems to be asking for here is a clear thesis statement. In a later conference on this same paper, he writes, next to the last sentence of this paragraph, the comment: "What are you trying to prove? Thesis?" And at the end of this conference he writes on the back of the essay: "improve your thesis s" (i.e., thesis statement). Although TJ frames this problem as a problem with a particular sentence, it is the place in the essay that concerns him, the last sentence of the first paragraph, and what he expected to see in that place and did not, a thesis statement.

There is no clear indication that the student, ST, has at this point understood that this is what the RPQ is implying, although he gives what seems to be the expected answer, "no." He does, however, seem to have understood that TJ considered the last sentence problematic because it did not say what the paper is about. In his next revision, ST takes out the problematic sentence and replaces it with the following sentence: "All these situations could have possibly better outcomes if there was a law forcing bystander intervention." ST interprets the RPQ and subsequent talk to mean that his last sentence should provide the *topic* rather than the *thesis* of the paper. ST actually had a thesis statement later in the paper, at the beginning of the third paragraph: "In my personal opinion, the Good Samaritan law will not be successful and will not be the solution to our questions." TJ, however, does not seem to have registered this, perhaps because it was not in the place where he had expected to find a thesis statement.

The possibility of misinterpretation is increased by the way TJ frames the problem as being a problem with a specific sentence, rather than as a failure to include a thesis statement at that point in the essay. Because the RPQs seem to invite a *no* answer, without elaboration, and the student gives this invited answer, it is difficult for the teacher to gauge the extent of his understanding. This RPQ then was both too inexplicit for what the teacher wanted to convey, and it also failed to target the problem correctly. The student may have been better served if the teacher had drawn his attention to the already-existing thesis statement and suggested ways to strengthen it.

2.3 RPQ with non-aligning response

The next excerpt, from the same conference, shows ST disagreeing with the negative assertion conveyed by an RPQ. The RPQ (line 142), the first of two in the excerpt, plays a somewhat different role in that it is used contingently after a student clarification of the targeted text, and is used to refer back to the student talk rather than the student text. However, it performs a similar function of showing what is problematic about the problematized portion of text and conveying a solution.

The talk in this excerpt begins just after the talk in Excerpt 38. TJ turns to page 3 of ST's text, where he has written the second "So?" comment. In this paragraph, ST is discussing what he considers a flaw of the proposed "Good Samaritan law" which would prosecute bystanders who refuse to aid an accident or crime victim. He gives an example of a couple hurrying to the airport to catch a plane for their honeymoon. On their way they see an accident, but do not take any action. If they are cited for not stopping, they can always give an excuse like this: they were rushing to help their grandmother who was suffering from an asthma attack.

Chapter 4. Yes/no used in pedagogically specific practices

The problem focused on in this excerpt is again one of relevance, as indicated by the second "So?". TJ's point is that ST had failed to establish the relevance of his example to his thesis.

After turning to the second "So?" comment, TJ reads the portion of text immediately before the comment:

(39)   TJ/ST
```
101  TJ:     .h: ((clears throat))
102          (3.0) ((TJ turns pages of text))
103          an again here.
104          ((TJ points to text))
105          (1.0) ((TJ makes circular
106          gesture above text))
107          .h ((reading)) "although the
108          couple was there,=they could make
109          up an excuse like they had to
110          assist their grandmother because
111          she was suffering from an asthma
112          attack."
113          (1.5) ((TJ opens eyes wide,
114          gazes at ST))
115          yeah?
116  ST:     wul like
117          (0.2)
118          so lik- I was tryna say like-
119          (1.0)
120          that'll like (0.5)
121          get em off the hook.
122          (1.5)
123          try- (.) (el- u-) try ta get off
124          the hook. cause
125  TJ:     o[k,           ]
126  ST:     [ya know like] (0.2) they they
127          couldn't stop n help em.
128          (0.2)
129          like the law woulda said
130  TJ:     uh huh
131  ST:     ta do.=so .h ya know like (0.2)
132          the grandma was (involved),
133          asthma attack.
134          (0.2)
135          an like (0.2) um (0.5) that
136          woulda get em off the hook cause
137          then: how can the law punish
138          em.=cause (0.2) they're: rushing
```

```
139                ta help the grandparents.
140 TJ:            good idea.
141                (1.0) ((TJ: nod))
142         -->    [didja tell me that?
143                [((TJ gestures toward ST))
144                (1.5) ((TJ points to text))
145 ST:            think so,
146                (1.0) ((TJ eyegaze on text;
147                ST shifts eyegaze to TJ))
148 TJ:            um:.
149                (1.0) ((TJ & ST eyegaze on text;
150                TJ gestures w/ pen above text
151                from top to bottom of paragraph))
152         -->    is it clear?
153 ST:            no
```

TJ's reading of ST's text (lines 107–112), brings it into the sequence of talk, enabling him to perform a further action on it. When TJ then challenges the relevance of this portion of text ("yeah?", line 115), ST provides an explanation for how this portion of text is relevant to the rest of his paper (lines 116–139). TJ first positively evaluates the student's explanation, "good idea." (line 140), then asks an RPQ which refers anaphorically back to the student's explanation, using the pronoun "that": "didja tell me that?" (line 142), conveying "you *didn't* tell me, in your text, what you just said orally, but you *should* have." In this case the RPQ criticizes the text by pointing out what is missing from the text: this very explanation. During another conference with a different student, the same teacher uses a similar RPQ, and in this case, makes the *should* explicit. The RPQ is shown in lines 3 and 10 with the single-headed arrow, and the *should* in lines 12–13 with the double-headed arrow.

(40) **TJ/SH**
```
01 TJ:             good answer.
02                 (0.8)
03 TJ:      -->    is that here yet?
04                 (1.5)
05 SH:             excuse me?
06 TJ:             is that- what you just said?
07 SH:             uh [huh,
08 TJ:                [is an excellent answer.
09 SH:             uh huh.
10 TJ:      -->    (          here yet)?
11 SH:             no: I don't think [so.
12 TJ:      -->>                     [mm. it should
```

```
13          -->> be,
14               (.)
15   TJ:         I think it would make a great
16               ending.
17   SH:         tch okay. h
```

Schegloff (1988a) demonstrates how a noticing of a negative event, "you didn't get en icecream sanwich," can formulate a failure and be heard as a complaint. In a similar way, the negative assertion conveyed by the RPQ in Excerpt 39 formulates a failure, as if the teacher were saying "In this sentence, you failed to say, in your paper, what you just said orally." The failure to "tell me that" is a "relevant omission" (Schegloff 1988a), suggesting that if the student had included that explanation in his text, showing how that portion of text is relevant to the rest of the paper, the teacher would not have questioned its relevance.

Jacoby and Gonzales (2002) show how similar types of negative observations are used by the head physicist in a research team to provide feedback on the performance of conference presentation rehearsals done by other members of the research group. There is a striking similarity in both their placement in the sequence and in the action performed. But the physics lab negative observations are made in the form of statements rather than RPQs. In physics lab comment sessions, these negative observations, e.g., "you didn't say that", are also raised contingently in sequences that focus on problems of clarity in the past performance. The head physicist's negative observations similarly target something said by the presenter during the evaluation, or comment session, in order to clarify a portion of the previous talk criticized as unclear. They convey that what the presenter said in clarification during the comment session should have been said earlier in the talk itself. Negative observations used as performance feedback in physics labs thus similarly point to a failure to do an expected action and point to what should be communicated in a revised version of the performance.

In Excerpt 39, ST at first disagrees with the implication of the teacher's RPQ, that his text does not include what he had just given orally: "t̲hink so," (line 145). He does this disagreement in a clearly dispreferred manner, showing his orientation to it as a disagreement. It is substantially delayed (1.5 seconds), mitigated by the epistemic qualifier *think*, and also said tentatively with continuing intonation.

The teacher subsequently asks a second RPQ (line 152):

```
146              (1.0) ((TJ eyegaze on text;
147              ST shifts eyegaze to TJ))
148   TJ:        um:.
```

```
149            (1.0) ((TJ & ST eyegaze on text;
150            TJ gestures w/ pen above text
151            from top to bottom of paragraph))
152       --> is it clear?
```

This time the pronoun "it" refers to that portion of the student text in which the student claims he has explained the relevance. The teacher is conceding that the student may have explained, in his paper, the relevance of the portion of text being criticized, but it obviously wasn't clear, or he would not have asked the first question, "didja tell me that?" This RPQ is more difficult for the student to disagree with as it is framed from the reader's perspective, i.e., it is the reader who evaluates whether the text is clear. This question gets a clear and immediate aligning answer:

```
152            --> is it clear?
153 ST:         no
```

In fact, in this example, it was the student, not the teacher who was correct. The student had shown the relevance of his example earlier in the paper. The problem here was actually a misleading introduction to the paragraph in question. In the first sentence of this paragraph, ST suggests that the proposed law against bystander apathy cannot be enforced because it will be difficult to prove that a particular person actually saw the scene of the crime or accident: "The least important of the three flaws that would make the law unsuccessful is that the law can not assume any person at the scene will see the situation." However, the example he gives in the remainder of this paragraph suggests a different reason why the law will be difficult to enforce: that bystanders "can always come up with the world's best excuses to avoid being punished by law." But the reframing of TJ's RPQ, together with the strength of the preference structure, may have persuaded the student to eventually agree with the teacher. I return to this problem in Chapter 6.

2.4 RPQ sequence series

Because of the inexplicit nature of these pedagogical RPQs and the fact that learning occurs over time, it is helpful to explicate a series of RPQ sequences from the same conference that show the process through which a student comes to an understanding of a pedagogical point. The point, in this case, is learning what to include from outside sources.

The first excerpt in this series has been discussed in Chapter 2 as Excerpt 16 and in Chapter 3 as Excerpt 28. The earlier focus of analysis was on the *yes/no*

RPQ in line 87 and the *wh-* RPQ in line 89. Here I focus on the pedagogical RPQ in lines 83–84. A copy of the relevant portion of SD's text can be found in Chapter 2, Excerpt 15.

To briefly summarize, the student, SD, has chosen to work on the second draft of his paper in which he discusses Charles de Gaulle's leadership, using various theories of leadership from class readings. Prior to this excerpt, SD has already established that he will be discussing Charles de Gaulle in terms of Zaleznik's (1984) concept of *charismatic leadership* and Gardner's (1996) concept of *direct leadership*.

```
(41)   TC/SD:7
       61  TC:      ok. ((reading)) "according to de
       62                Gaulle" ((she meant "Gardner"))
       63                ↓here's what you say "according
       64                to de Gaulle leaders are char-
       65                categorized as direct indirect
       66                (0.2) ordinary innovative (0.8)
       67                or: visionary."↓
       68                (1.5) ((TC eyegaze on text;
       69                bent over text))
       70                why did you: talk about that.
       71                (0.8) ((TC moves paper toward SD;
       72                straightens body;
       73                eyegaze still on text))
       74  SD:      uh s- [cause (0.8) d- this one of
       75                  [((TC looks up briefly at
       76                SD, then down at text))
       77                the sources that we (.) read in
       78                cla[ss.
       79  TC:          [um [hum?
       80  SD:              [so I jus wanted ta include
       81                that. as uh: information.
       82                (0.5) ((TC eyegaze on SD))
       83  TC:   --> Is it relevant?
       84         --> *to what you're saying?
       85                (0.8)* ((*SD looks down))
       86  SD:      No it's just background. heh h
       87  TC:      It's background?=
       88  SD:      =yeah.=
       89  TC:      ok how's it background.=because I-
       90                like .h most people wouldn't
       91                know[:
       92  SD:          [((sniff))
       93  TC:      maybe what he meant by direct
```

```
94              indirect ordinary innovative or
95              visionary.
96    SD:       (yeah.)/(well) ok,
97              (1.5) ((SD nods))
```

As discussed in Chapter 2, there are two issues being worked through here. One is that SD has introduced many leadership terms from Gardner: "direct, indirect, ordinary, innovative, and visionary," most of which are not relevant to his essay on de Gaulle. Only the first, "direct" leadership, is relevant. The second issue is one of *recipient design* (Sacks et al. 1974): SD has introduced the terms without defining them, as if writing for the teacher or other members of his class. He was supposed to be writing for an audience unfamiliar with the class readings.

TC first reads the problematic portion of SD's text (lines 61–67) and asks him to provide an account for including this material (line 70). This can already convey to SD that TC considers this portion of text problematic. As discussed earlier, SD warrants including this information because it was from the class readings (lines 74–81), treating this paper as if it were an essay exam whose purpose was to show the teacher that he had done the reading.

When then TC asks, "Is it relevant? to what you're saying?" (lines 83–84), in a context where both TC and SD have already discussed the fact that most of these characteristics of leadership are not relevant, this question, like the RPQs in Excerpts 38–40, conveys a strong epistemic stance, a negative assertion. TC seems to be reminding SD that this information is not relevant to what SD has just agreed he was focusing on in his paper.

SD's response to this RPQ is mixed. In spite of the .8 second pause (line 85), it is begun as an aligning response, with a clear, unmitigated "no" (line 86). SD displays agreement with TC's criticism that what he has written is not relevant to what he is saying about de Gaulle. However, TC's RPQ, which shows why that portion of text is problematic, also implies a solution, provided that the student is familiar with the norms of American academic written discourse being oriented to here, i.e., "If it's not relevant, it should be removed from the text." However, SD does not appear to agree with or understand the implied solution: that the information should be eliminated. He adds an utterance which suggests he had some proper reasons for including this information: "it's just background. heh h" (line 86).

TC first deals with this misunderstanding of *background*, i.e., SD has introduced the terms without defining them for the reader (lines 87–95; see discussion of Excerpt 16, Chapter 4 and Excerpt 28, Chapter 3). After further discussion of the relationship between *direct* and *charismatic* leadership, TC returns to SD's use of the term "background":

(42) TC/SD:12
```
193 TC:      That's fine ta do it that way.=
194          um: (0.5) .h but when yer- (2.8)
195          when yer um: (1.0) mentioning
196          this background information?=like
197          you called it background
198          in[formation, .hh ya
199 SD:         [yeah,
200 TC:      know: (.) [try ta think about- ]
201 SD: -->            [I have ta explain   ]
202     --> (it)/(them)?
203 TC:      .h well: (.) explain it an- but
204          um: (0.2) (>ah mean<) ya don need
205          (0.5) it's background information
206          [so ya can be general.           ]
207 SD:      [I don hafta mention every sin]gle
208          one right?
209 TC:      right.
210 SD:      o:k
```

In the above excerpt SD seems to be displaying that he has understood both problems originally targeted by TC; when he introduces terms from the readings, he has to explain them:

```
201 SD: -->            [I have ta explain   ]
202     --> (it)/(them)?
```

and he doesn't need to include every one of the terms:

```
207 SD:      [I don hafta mention every sin]gle
208          one right?
```

However, as the interaction continues, SD's understanding, or his agreement with TC, proves less firm. In the next excerpt, TC establishes that relevant background to include from the class readings for this section of the essay would be a discussion of Gardner's concept of *direct leadership*, contrasting the concept with *indirect leadership*. But, in another RPQ (lines 224–226), she questions SD's reference to the Zaleznik and Wills readings in this part of the essay:

(43) TC/SD:13-15
```
211 TC:      you can- (.) it's background
212          in[formation=
213 SD:        [((sniff))
```

```
214  TC:      =so you can be general.=like you
215           can explain general1y what a direct
216           leader i:s?
217  SD:      °kay?°
218  TC:      as opposed to an indirect leader?
219           according to Gardner?
220           (1.0) ((TC eyegaze on paper))
221  TC:      um:
222           (1.0) ((TC eyegaze on paper))
223  SD:      [((sniff sniff))
224  TC: -->  [But do you think you really need
225           to talk about Zaleznik and Will:s
226           right here. ((TC points to paper))
227           (1.8) ((TC & SD: eyegaze on
228           paper))
229  TC:      As far [as (0.2) if you're thinking
230                 [((TC looks up at SD))
231           [about (saying)]
232  SD:      [I include um because] the: tho-
233           these are the sources that we read
234           in class.
235  TC:      mm hmm. [oh I see.]
236  SD:             [that's- tha- that was] the
237           reason.
238           (0.2)
239  TC:      ok.
240           (0.2)
```

This RPQ, "But do you think you really need to talk about Zaleznik and Will:s right here." (lines 224–226), differs from the others in that it includes an element in its design, the word *really*, which may predispose the question toward a *no* answer (cf. Heritage 2002a). In this respect, it is similar to MacNeil's yes/no RPQ challenge in Excerpt 10: "powell suggested the king would be able to rally. (0.5) the different elements. *will he really*,=because …". The implication of TC's question, based on SD's stated intention to begin his paper with a discussion of Gardner's concept of direct leadership, is that SD should not have included Zaleznik and Wills at this point in his essay.

Rather than giving the preferred response to TC's question, demonstrating his understanding that he doesn't need to include all the sources he has read at this point, SD gives a dispreferred response in a dispreferred manner. SD disagrees by once again justifying his inclusion of all the authors from the readings: "I include um because the: tho- these are the sources that we read in class. that's- tha- that was the reason." (lines 232–234, 236–237). This justification is substantially delayed, delivered in overlap with TC's next turn which itself began after a pause of 1.8 seconds.

There is also a different type of lack of alignment between the teacher's question and the student's response. The teacher asks "But do you t̲hink you really need to talk about Zaleznik and Will:s *right here*." and the student responds: "I̲ in̲clude um because …". The teacher is asking about discussing Zaleznik and Wills *at that particular point* in the essay, but the student responds with a justification of why he included them in the essay at all. He did not put them in *at this particular point*; he merely put them in the paper. He seemingly has not yet understood the difference between putting them in the paper *at a particular point* and simply putting them anywhere in the paper, which is one of the lessons TC is trying to teach him. Similarly, SD did not put them in the paper because he needed to *talk about* them but because he needed to *include* them, which reflects his orientation toward a requirement to show what he has remembered from the readings. This is the same orientation he showed in Excerpt 41, an orientation which was directly dealt with in the previous interaction.

TC then goes on to make explicit what SD needs to do: only include what the reader needs to know to follow SD's argument, and she exemplifies this by reading SD a good example from his own text:

```
241        so think of it more as background
242        informa[tion.]
243  SD:          [°(yeah ok.)/(background)°]
244  TC:   that's really r̲elevant,
245        (0.2)
246  TC:   I mean- (0.2) only: (0.2) what they
247        need to know, (0.2) right then.
248        (0.5)
249        cause y̲ou could even bring Zaleznik
250        in l̲ater. [like you were saying=
251  SD:             [°ok°
252  TC:   =you wanted to do. .h so- t̲hink of
253        it as being-
254        [(0.5) ok. (1.8)                    ]
255        [((TC looking up as if thinking))]
256        w̲hat will help my reader to follow
257        the rest of what I'm gonna say.=
258        just g̲eneral inform̲ation.
259        (1.0)
260  SD:   [((sniff sniff))
261  TC:   [So I think that's maybe what-
```

```
262          (0.2) ((TC picks up pen))
263          what goes in here.
264          (0.8) ((TC begins writing))
265  TC:    °um:°
266          (12.0) ((writing on paper: "make
267          this into backgrd";
268          then reading silently))
269          °mkay° so- an ya want it ta be:
270          (3.0) relevant.
271          (5.2) ((writing on paper:
272          "relevant"; reading silently))
273  TC:    see- [and then you did this really=
274              [((TC moves hand w/ pen to
275          point to 3rd paragraph of essay))
276          =well. see: (1.0) ((reading)) "One
277          particular trait of the leaders is
278          that they're usually recognized
279          during hard times." So
280          [that- that's .h=
281          [((TC moves eyegaze to SD))
282  SD:    [°(yeah)
283  TC:    (0.5) the leadership, (0.8)
284          explanati- in the explanation for
285          leadership,=an then you talk about
286          (0.2) how de Gaulle (2.0) fit
287          that (1.0) explanation.
288          [ok?]
289  SD:    [°(um hum)°]
```

The final example of an RPQ sequence targeting a similar problem occurs much later in the same conference. In this excerpt TC is advising SD to combine two of his paragraphs into one. The first paragraph describes SD's feelings of sympathy for de Gaulle. The next paragraph introduces Zaleznik's theory of charismatic leadership and discusses how a charismatic leader attracts followers who sympathize with his cause. In that second paragraph, however, SD has included information on Zaleznik's theory of *consensus leadership*. TC is criticizing SD's inclusion of the concept of *consensus leadership* as irrelevant.

(44)   TC/SD:20

```
411  TC:    so maybe this is actually one
412          paragraph here.
413          (0.8) ((TC eyegaze on SD;
414          SD eyegaze on paper))
415  SD:    [°ok.°
```

```
416  TC:      [I mean it flows really well
417           together. right?
418  SD:      °ok.° [( )
419                 [like you're talking about
420           [your emotion:s,
421           [((TC gestures: two hands open,
422           palms facing each other on table))
423           (0.8) ((TC holds gesture, eyegaze
424           on hands))
425           an:d
426           [(0.2)] an here if you describe
427           [((TC moves pen toward paper))]
428           [(0.5)
429           [((TC gestures with pen toward
430           paper))
431           the charismatic leadership a little
432           more:,
433           (6.5) / ((TC eyegaze on paper))
434           see::,
435           (1.0) / ((TC eyegaze on paper))
436  TC:      here you're talking about
437           <satisfying the needs>.
438           (1.0)
439           and sympathai- (0.2) sympathizing
440           with the leader's cause:.
441           (1.8) ((TC eyegaze on paper))
442           that's what a charismatic leader
443           (2.0) causes in his followers.
444           right. ok (.) so
445           (2.5) ((TC eyegaze on paper))
446           ↑why do you talk a↑bout consensus
447           leadership here.
448  SD:      (th)cause that was the other thing
449           that (0.2) Zaleznik talked about.
450           (hh)=
451  TC:      =um hum[:
452  SD:             [besides (.) uh charismatic
453           leadership.=
454  TC: -->  =are you gonna talk about it?=in
455           relation to: de Gaulle?
456  SD:      (this) nuh uh. heh (h)=
457  TC:      =not right here, right?=
458  SD:      =uh uh.
459  TC:      yeah.=
```

After summarizing the portion of text that relates to charismatic leadership and accepting it, lines 436–444, there is a pause, where TC displays continued attention to the text. She ends this pause with a question in lines 446–447: "↑Why do you talk a↑bout con̲sensus l̲eadership here." With this question the teacher both introduces a different portion of student text into the talk, the "talk about consensus leadership" and, at the same time, targets it as possibly problematic by asking the student to justify why he has included it in that paragraph, making that inclusion accountable.

SD once again answers her question by giving a justification for including a discussion of this term in his essay (lines 448–450, 452–453): "(th)cause that was the other thing that (0.2) Zaleznik t̲alked about. (hh) besides (.) uh charismatic l̲eadership." This is now the third time that SD has given a similar justification for including (from the teacher's perspective) irrelevant source material in the essay.

TC again uses an RPQ to question the relevance of the portion of text she has just problematized (lines 454–455) : "=are you gonna talk about it?=in relation to: de Gaulle?" The pronoun "it" in line 454 refers anaphorically back to the portion of student text summarized in lines 446–447 as "talk about consensus leadership." In constructing the RPQ, the teacher uses a phrase from the student's answer, "talk about", and puts contrastive stress on "you̲" to contrast the student's focus for his paper with his account for why he included this information, "(th)cause that was the other thing that (0.2) Zaleznik t̲alked about. (hh)".

Like the other RPQs, in this context, it conveys a negative assertion: "You're *not* gonna talk about it in relation to de Gaulle." TC has read the paper, and, in their talk just prior to this excerpt, SD and TC have discussed the focus of the paper: de Gaulle's charismatic leadership. She knows, and SD knows that she knows, that he does not intend to include a discussion of *consensus leadership* in his paper. The RPQ also conveys a solution: e.g., "If you're not going to talk about it in relation to de Gaulle, it should not be included in the paragraph."

SD gives the equivalent of a *no* answer to TC's question, (line 456) aligning with the stance displayed in the RPQ: "(this) n̲uh uh. heh (h)". The negative answer is done in a clearly preferred manner: directly, without pause or mitigation, demonstrating his orientation to *no* as the preferred response. There is a slight laugh token at the end of SD's utterance, which could also suggest agreement with TC's criticism. As was pointed out in the discussion of Excerpt 16 in Chapter 2 (Excerpt 41 in this Chapter), SD produces similar short laugh tokens throughout the conference at places in the interaction that could be potentially embarrassing for him. Here he could be demonstrating embarrassment at having this lack of relevance pointed out to him, especially since this is the third time in this conference that TC has brought up the relevance problem.

TC also shows an orientation to *no* as a preferred answer in the way that she responds to SD's answer. She agrees with the answer rather than treating it as new information (lines 457 and 459):

```
454  TC:       =are you gonna talk about it?=in
455            relation to: de Gaulle?
456  SD:       (this) nuh uh. heh (h)=
457  TC:  -->  =not right here, right?=
458  SD:       =uh uh.
459  TC:  -->  yeah.=
```

In this response TC treats her question as a *known-information* question, not a "real" question, requesting information. It would be odd to agree with new information one has just requested.

TC's response in line 457 also adds the question of placement: "not *right here*, right?" This reinforces the point she was making earlier, when discussing the relevance of including Zaleznik and Wills *at that point* in the essay: "But do you think you really need to talk about Zaleznik and Will:s *right here*." (Excerpt 43, lines 224–226). SD again gives a preferred, agreeing response, in a preferred manner (line 458), and the sequence ends in mutual alignment, with TC's agreement (line 459).

In the course further discussion, both SD (line 623) and TC (lines 625–635) make explicit what the earlier RPQ had suggested implicitly: that SD eliminate the material on consensus leadership:

```
615  TC:   so wul what about
616        this: charismatic leadership
617        [thing.=do you think it relates to
618        [((underlines "charismatic
619        leadership" in paper))
620        what you've just said before?=
621  SD:   =yeah?
622        (0.5)
623        but not (.) consensus,
624        (0.8)
625  TC:   ok. consensus (0.5) not really.=
626        right?=
627  SD:   =ye[ah
628  TC:      [((brackets section in paper on
629        consensus [leadership))
630                  [consensus maybry (0.5)
631        maybe isn't (.) the most relevant
```

```
632          thing right here. .h so let's look
633          at this paragraph then, .h let's
634          pretend that consensus stuff is
635          go:[ne.
636 SD:      [ok,
```

In this conference, SD was having trouble reconciling two opposing concepts (1) TC's implication that material not relevant to his discussion of de Gaulle should be eliminated, and (2) SD's own orientation to this essay as a place to show the teacher that he has done the readings. Unlike the RPQs in the TJ/ST Excerpts, 38 and 39, the first RPQ sequence in this series, Excerpt 41, did not close off further discussion but engendered it. In addition, TC followed the final RPQ sequence with explicit advice to delete the irrelevant material, making the information implicit in the RPQ explicit. However, in spite of this lengthy discussion, the problem that SD was having in was not directly dealt with or fully resolved in this conference, nor in SD's following draft. In the following draft the student made the change suggested by the last RPQ (Excerpt 44), but not by the earlier ones. The complexity of the idea, given that the student was operating with a different concept of the purpose of this essay, took more than one conference to deal with. By the final draft, the earlier problems were also solved.

2.5 Sequence and question design

The pedagogical RPQ sequences discussed above generally unfold in the following manner:

1. *A portion of the student text is introduced into the talk and is characterized as problematic.*

These RPQs occur in sequences which target for criticism a particular portion of the marked up student text in front of the participants. The portion of text targeted for criticism needs to be incorporated into the sequence of talk before other actions can be performed on it. Teachers do this through the following practices. First, they direct the student's visual orientation to that portion of text by means of gesture and/or deictic reference: e.g., "'sus look at this.", or "an again here." (cf. Goodwin 1986). They then animate the student's words (Goffman 1981), bringing the relevant portion of student text into the sequence of talk by reading it aloud, paraphrasing it, or summarizing it. In the process of transforming the student text into talk, it is often framed to set it off from the surrounding talk. The framing is accomplished by the same utterance that directs student attention to the relevant portion of text, e.g., "an again here." Sometimes a more explicit *reported speech* frame is used, e.g., "↓here's what you say." The last example also shows how changes in pitch, i.e., a pitch calibrated lower than surrounding talk, can frame the portion of student text that is read.

Either prior to or immediately after the introduction of student text into the talk, and before the RPQ is asked, it is made clear that there is something problematic about that portion of text. The way in which this is done varies. For example, in Excerpt 44 the teacher asked the student to justify why he had included the portion of text under discussion, "↑Why do you talk a↑bout consensus leadership here." (lines 446–447), making the inclusion of that portion of text accountable and suggesting that there is a problem with it. The RPQs in Excerpt 38 are part of a sequence which is explicating the teacher's comment, "So?", written on the essay. It is already clear from the comment that the teacher considers the portion of text adjacent to the written comment problematic, and it is also made clear that the ensuing talk will be explicating the comment and, in consequence, explaining the problem.

2. *An RPQ is asked by the teacher.*

The RPQs are all yes/no questions with upward intonation. Like many of the RPQs discussed earlier, there is no special intonation that would distinguish them from information-seeking yes/no questions. As we have seen, they are used after a portion of student text previously brought into the sequence of talk has been characterized as problematic. The RPQs refer back to that text, or to a preceding student utterance about that text, by using a pronoun: "that" or "it," to establish anaphoric co-reference to either that portion of the student text or to the preceding student utterance. In the context in which they are asked, they convey an assertion of the opposite polarity to that of the question: a negative assertion, e.g., "=are you gonna talk about it?=in relation to: de Gaulle?" conveys "You're *not* going to talk about it in relation to de Gaulle". This negative assertion acts as a veiled criticism of the student text, showing the student why that text is problematic (e.g.: "It's not relevant to the focus of your paper") and indirectly suggests a remedy (e.g.: "If it's not relevant, leave it out").

3. *The student's answer displays a preference for agreement with the stance displayed in the RPQ.*

Earlier I suggested that answers to RPQs prefer agreement with the stance, or implied assertion, displayed in the question, and it is *in this way* that they agree with the preference of the question. These RPQs, however, have a more complex preference structure than the preference for a certain answer that aligns with the stance conveyed by the question. Some types of first pair parts can function as "actions in their own right and as vehicles or formats for other actions" (Schegloff 1995b: 75, to appear). Yes/no questions, in particular, seem especially useful in this respect. As vehicles for other actions, they can have multiple preferences: one for answering the question and one for responding to the action that the question is being used to perform (Schegloff 1995b, to appear). Because the RPQs in these sequences are used as vehicles for pointing out what is problematic about a portion of student text, acting as veiled criticisms, there is a second preference structure operating with these questions: a preference for responding to the criticism conveyed by the RPQ.

Although there may not normally be a preference for agreeing with criticism of one's performance (and thus of one's competence) in ordinary conversation, in the writing conferences, the criticisms are being used to assist the performance of students who are just beginning to learn a new genre and are not expected to be competent in that genre. Criticism may, in fact, be one way that participants are socialized into becoming experts in a new genre.[31] Disagreeing with the teacher's criticism at this stage in the learning process may be seen as inappropriately defensive, as calling the expertise of the teacher into question.[32] If this is the case and agreement with the teacher's criticism is, indeed, the preferred response, the two preference structures of the RPQs would be congruent. The preference for agreement suggests that a *no* response would align with the negative assertion conveyed by the RPQ. This agreement with the negative assertion would also accept the criticism conveyed by the RPQ.

As we have seen, students do display an orientation to both a preference for agreement with the negative assertion and to aligning with the criticism of their performance. When answering RPQs in these sequences, students treat them as *no-preferring*. The majority of answers are either *no* or its equivalent. When students answer "no", their answers have many of the characteristics of a preferred response. Answers are generally direct, without mitigation, demonstrating an orientation to *no* as the preferred response.

As we saw in Excerpts 39 and 43, students do not always agree with the assertion conveyed by the RPQ, but when they disagree, they orient to their disagreement *as being* a disagreement by doing it in a dispreferred manner: indirectly or with mitigation, substantially delayed and sometimes with accounts for disagreeing. This dispreferred manner, in turn, demonstrates their orientation to the RPQ as conveying an assertion that can be agreed or disagreed with.

4. *The teacher's response displays the preference structure of the question.*

Teachers' responses to students' answers also orient to the RPQs' preference for an aligning *no*. When a student gives a dispreferred answer, the teacher may correct the misconceptions in that answer, or even redesign the question to achieve a preferred response, as done in the portion of Excerpt 39 reprinted below. As discussed earlier, the teacher responded to a dispreferred answer by reanalyzing the problem in a second RPQ, designed to get a preferred answer (line 152). This time the student gives an aligning answer in a preferred manner (line 153):

Reprint of (39)
```
142            [didja tell me that?
143            [(((TJ gestures toward ST))
144            (1.5) ((TJ points to text))
145 ST:        think so,
146            (1.0) ((TJ eyegaze on text;
147            ST shifts eyegaze to TJ))
148 TJ:        um:.
149            (1.0) ((TJ & ST eyegaze on text;
150            TJ gestures w/ pen above text
151            from top to bottom of paragraph))
152       -->  is it clear?
153 ST:   -->  no
```

Participants in conversation often take steps to "maximize the occurrence of a sequence with a preferred second pair part" (Schegloff, 1995b: 79, to appear). This can be done by redoing a first pair part after a brief pause that may forecast that a dispreferred response is on the way. It can also be done through a presequence. For example, a pre-invitation such as "Say what 'r you doing.", given at the beginning of a telephone call, may receive a blocking response, "Well, we're going out.", which enables the initiator to avoid doing an invitation which would likely be rejected, a dispreferred response (Schegloff 1995b: 24–25, to appear). In Excerpt 39, the fact that the teacher redid the RPQ to get a preferred answer, even after the first RPQ received a dispreferred answer, is evidence that the teacher is orienting to its preference for a *no* answer.

When a preferred answer is given, the teacher may agree with that answer, as in lines 457 and 459 in the portion of Excerpt 44, reprinted below:

Reprint of (44)
```
454  TC:           =are you gonna talk about it?=in
455                relation to: de Gaulle?
456  SD:           (this) nuh uh. heh (h)=
457  TC:    -->    =not right here, right?=
458  SD:           =uh uh.
459  TC:    -->    yeah.=
```

The teacher's agreement with the student's answer shows that her RPQ was not asking for information, but was seeking confirmation of an implied negative assertion.

In Excerpt 38, the RPQ (line 51) receives a preferred answer that is validated as correct by the teacher :

Reprint of (38)
```
51  TJ:          [is that what this paper's about?
52               [((TJ moves head to side as if to
53               meet ST's eyegaze))
54               (0.8)
55  ST:          no:,
56               (0.5)
57  TJ:   -->    right.*
58               (0.2)
59               that's the problem.
60               (1.8) ((TJ & ST mutual eyegaze;
61               TJ smiles))
```

The teacher's "right." (line 57) characterizes the RPQ as a *known-information* question by suggesting that there was a "right" answer to it. This again supports that the teacher had an expected answer in mind. In all of these responses, we see the teacher orienting to the implied assertion originally displayed in the RPQ.

2.6 How these RPQs are interpreted as RPQs

We have seen how both teachers and students display an orientation to these RPQs as preferring *no* as an answer. I have suggested that this preference is based on a preference for alignment, or agreement, with the implied negative assertion displayed by the question. Yet, like many of the yes/no and wh- question RPQs discussed in Chapters 2 and 3, there is nothing in the design of most of these RPQs which either projects an epistemic stance or predisposes the question to prefer *no* as an answer. None of these RPQs contain negative forms, such as the negatively-formatted questions from news interviewers, or negative polarity items, which could suggest a possibility of interpreting them as reversed polarity negative assertions. Neither are they said with special prosodic marking, e.g.:

(45)
```
Are you gonna talk about it?=in relation to: de
   Gaulle?
Didja tell me that?
Is it clear?
Is that here yet?
Is that what this paper's about?
```

Taken in isolation, these questions would appear to be simple yes/no questions asking for information. How then do these questions convey assertions? Like the previous RPQ challenges, they can be understood as RPQs not by any elements in their question design, but by the student's taking into account two elements of their context: (1) the questioner's state of knowledge vis-à-vis the question, and (2) the trajectory of action established in the sequence and the RPQ's placement in that trajectory of action.

1. *The questioner's known state of knowledge.*

When asking an RPQ, the teachers are not asking for information that they do not have. When the teacher asks "didja tell me that?", he has already read and commented on the paper and knows, or thinks he knows, that the student didn't "tell him that." And when the teacher asks "Are you gonna talk about it?=in relation to: de Gaulle?", the student and teacher have already discussed what the student will be focusing on in his paper, specifically that he will be discussing de Gaulle in terms of *charismatic* but not *consensus* leadership. As discussed earlier, this may be one way in which RPQs in general are understood as RPQs: prior to asking the RPQ it has already been established, either from the immediate linguistic context or from the extra-linguistic context, that the questioner has access to the information which answers the question, and it is in this way that RPQs are heard as epistemic stance displays rather than as information-seeking questions.

2. *The trajectory of action.*

The second element in the context that enables the student to interpret these RPQs as RPQs is the trajectory of action established in the sequence prior to the RPQ. This trajectory of action helps participants determine what the RPQ is being used to do. As explained earlier, participants in conversation interpret utterances based on their understanding of what preceded those utterances and the course of action that the preceding utterances seem to be implementing. They ask the question: "Why that now?" (Schegloff & Sacks 1973). Prior to each RPQ, a portion of student text is introduced into the talk and characterized as problematic. It is at this point that the RPQ is asked, referring back to that portion of text targeted as problematic. In each case, if the answer to the RPQ were "yes", it would suggest that there was nothing problematic about the text. If the question conveyed, however, a negative assertion, it would both show what is problematic about the text and imply a solution. For example in Excerpt 44, after problematizing a portion of student text by asking the student to justify its inclusion, "↑Why do you talk a↑bout consensus leadership here.", the teacher asks "=are you gonna talk about it?=in relation to: de Gaulle?" The reminder that the student is *not* going to talk about consensus leadership in relation to de Gaulle shows why the discussion of consensus leadership is problematic. Similarly, "didja tell me that?" and "is it clear?" in Excerpt 39 are also asked after problematizing a portion of text. The teacher in this case is explicating a large question mark he put in the margin of the text, criticizing the relevance of that portion of the text to the thesis of the paper. The first RPQ refers to the student's explanation of why that portion of text was, indeed, relevant; the second one refers to his text. In each case, if the answers to the questions were "yes", there would be nothing problematic about the student text under discussion here, and no reason to ask the questions at this point. There is thus a sense that the teacher is conveying a *no* answer to these questions, the only answer which would further the course of problem-solving action begun in this sequence. Of course, the student can answer "yes," disagreeing with the suggestion that there is something problematic about the text. But for the teacher to ask "is it clear?", conveying the possibility that the portion of text he had just characterized as problematic was, in fact, clear, would make no sense in this sequential context. Only a negative assertion, "It's not clear," would further the course of action established at the beginning of the sequence.

3 RPQs used as hints in grammar correction sequences

3.1 Introduction

In the preceding section I discussed grammatically affirmative yes/no RPQs used to help students find problems with organization and content in their drafts, ensuring that the student is able to solve these problems in a future revision. In those sequences, both teachers and students display an orientation to *no* or its equivalent as the preferred answer.

This section focuses on RPQs used in sequences where teachers are assisting students to self-correct grammar errors. As in the above segments, the RPQs are used to show why a portion of student text or student talk is problematic and point to a solution. However, as I will show, the RPQs play a different role in these sequences, and this differing role engenders a different preference structure.

3.2 Preference structure of RPQs as hints

As we saw earlier, certain kinds of first pair parts, especially yes/no questions, can function "both as actions in their own right and as vehicles or formats for other actions" (Schegloff 1995b: 75, to appear). For example, a question such as "Would you like a cup of coffee?" can function both as a question, (i.e., request for information) and an offer. In such cases the question, as a first pair part, would have two sets of preferences: one for the format: the question, and the other for the action implemented through it: the offer. This is also the case with the RPQs described earlier in this chapter. They ask a question that conveys a negative assertion and, as such, prefers agreement with that assertion. The question, with its implied negative assertion is also a vehicle through which teachers criticize a portion of student text, showing why it is problematic and pointing to a solution. These RPQs have two sets of preferences: one for answering the question in a way that aligns with the assertion conveyed through the question, a second for responding to the criticism, the action done through the question. These preferences are congruent: a *no* answer both aligns with the implicit negative assertion and also accepts the criticism conveyed by the RPQ.

Sometimes when first pair parts have multiple preferences, the relevant responses for each of the actions differ. In these cases, the format is usually responded to first and the action second. For example, a response of "Yes, thank you" to "Would you like a cup of coffee?" first answers the question with "yes" and then accepts the offer with "thank you." (Schegloff 1995b, to appear). Certain questions with multiple preferences, if answered with the preferred answer, make a course of action relevant, e.g., "Kin I hev yer light?", or, in a telephone conversation, "Is Judy there?" Merely giving an affirmative answer would be incomplete as this answer deals only with the format, the question, without dealing with the action for which the question was a vehicle, the request. The relevant action, in this case the granting of the request, needs to be supplied. For example:

(46) SB, 1[33]
```
01 All:       Hello?
02 Joh:       Yeah, is Judy there?
03 All:  -->  Yeah, just a second.
04            ((silence))
05 Jud:       Hello,
```

"Is Judy there?" both asks a question and requests that the recipient bring Judy to the phone, if the answer to the question is "yes." Allen's "yeah" in line 3 answers the question; this affirmative answer makes an action relevant: complying with the request. "Just a second" shows that John's request is being complied with.

Supplying the action without giving a *yes* answer would, however, not be considered incomplete or inappropriate, as shown in the following example:

(47) **New Year's Invitation**
```
01             ((dial tone rings, twice))
02 Mom:        Hel:lo.
03 Bon:        .hhh hello may I speak ta Jim
04             please?
05 Mom:  -->   Just a minute.
06             (2.0)
07             ((off the line)) JIM
08             (7.0)
09 Jim:        Hello,
```

There is no *yes* answer to the question, merely a response to the request demonstrating that the request is being complied with (line 5). Jim is then called and comes to the phone.

The RPQs in the sequences I discuss in this section share the same actions as those described earlier in this chapter and thereby invoke the same set of preferences. They ask a question, which conveys a negative assertion and, as such, prefers agreement with that assertion. The question, with its implied negative assertion, is also a vehicle through which teachers criticize a portion of student text or talk, showing why it is problematic and pointing to a solution. However, this implied negative assertion and the criticism done through it is, in these sequences, a vehicle for a third action: giving a hint to enable the students to perform an ongoing course of action correctly.

In each of the two sequences analyzed below, a course of action has already been established: eliciting a knowledge display from the student. In one example, this knowledge display takes the form of self-correcting a grammar error; in the other, it consists of naming verb phrases in preparation for student self-correction of errors. The RPQ is used in each case when the student displays trouble in accomplishing the required action. The RPQ, by conveying a negative assertion, acts as a hint to enable the student to perform the knowledge display correctly. In one example, where the student has been naming verb phrases in a sentence of his text, the RPQ is used to prompt the student to correct an incomplete answer. In the second example the RPQ is used to assist the student to provide a self-correction of a grammar error in his text when that student seems to be having trouble finding the error.

Because a course of action has already been established, and the RPQ is used when students show evidence of trouble performing that action correctly, the preference structure for these sequences is somewhat different from that of the sequences discussed earlier. The students in the two excerpts below do not respond to the format or to the criticism by answering the question, as in the earlier sequences; rather, they orient to the action which the RPQ is performing: a hint to enable them to complete their performance correctly. In the first excerpt the student responds to the hint by returning to his text and correcting his previous answer. In the second excerpt, where the student is demonstrating trouble finding an error in his text, the RPQ does not do its job of assisting the student to find the error, yet the student orients to the RPQ as if it were asked to assist him with his performance: he demonstrates continued attention to the problematic sentence by whispering it to himself, as if he were engaged in searching for the error. In these two examples, the preference for performing the relevant action dominates over the preference for answering the question to such an extent that the first preference is not addressed.

3.3 Analysis of RPQ hints

The following excerpt is part of a larger activity during which the teacher, TJ, models a strategy for the student, ST, to use on his own to self-correct the verb errors in his draft. The activity begins with a series of questions that prompt ST to identify verb phrases in the first two sentences of his text. As ST identifies each one, TJ highlights it. When all the verb phrases in the two sentences have been identified, ST begins correcting the verb errors in the highlighted phrases, one by one.

Excerpt 49 occurs near the beginning of this activity when TJ is getting ST to identify verb phrases in the first sentence. Here is the first sentence of ST's uncorrected text (bolded portions represent highlighting which has already been done by TJ at this point in the conference):

(48) ST Text

In the article "Beyond the reach of law" a tragedy **happen** to a young man who's life could have been saved if other **were willing to help him**.

ST has just identified two of the verbs (highlighted by the teacher) in the first sentence and is now offering a third, "saved", in response to TJ's "a:nd?":

(49) TJ/ST:4
```
49  TJ:       a:nd?
50            (0.5) ((ST & TJ: eyegaze on text))
51  ST:       [saved?
52            (0.8) ((ST & TJ: eyegaze on text;
53            partway through pause, TJ moves
54            pen toward text))
55  TJ:       [saved?
56            [((TJ highlights text))
57  ST:       °yeah
58       -->  just saved?
59            (0.2)
60  ST:       oh. could have been saved.
61  TJ:       [*there ya go.* ((*creaky voice))
62            [((TJ begins to highlight text))
63            (1.2) ((TJ finishes highlighting
64            text))
65            ok. next sentence.
```

ST's answer (line 51) is given with upward intonation, as if for confirmation. TJ confirms ST's answer by highlighting it and repeating it, again with upward intonation (lines 55–56). Even though this repeat is done with upward intonation as if it were initiating a repair (Schegloff et al. 1977), TJ seems to be using this repetition to register receipt of ST's answer (Schegloff 1997a)[34] rather than as a repair to confirm his hearing of the answer, as the repeat is simultaneous with his highlighting of it. He does not wait for a confirmation to highlight it. This highlighting suggests an acceptance of the answer as at least partially cor-

Chapter 4. Yes/no used in pedagogically specific practices 103

rect. ST, however, seems to be interpreting the upward intonation as eliciting confirmation of a hearing; he confirms the hearing with "yeah" (line 57).

But ST's answer is incomplete. Because TJ will be eliciting correction of verb tense errors, he needs to elicit the finite verbs in the text and highlight them. ST has given only the non-finite portion of the verb phrase, the past participle "saved." Rather than correcting ST by adding the missing finite portion of the verb phrase, TJ prompts ST to self-correct his answer. He does this with an RPQ: "just saved?" (line 58).

This question is an RPQ in that it implies a negative assertion: "The verb phrase is not *just* 'saved'; there's more". Like the previous RPQs studied, this RPQ refers back to something in the student's text or talk, in this case, the student's answer. Also like the previous RPQs, this RPQ both implies what is problematic about the student's answer and points to a solution. The question suggests to ST the possibility that his answer was inadequate and needs correction and also tells what kind of correction needs to be made, i.e., an addition to the word "saved."

Unlike the previous RPQs, however, this RPQ does not get *no* as an answer. The student responds only to its action as a hint. Prior to this, a course of action has already been established: the student's naming of verb phrases in the first sentence of his essay, and the RPQ is used as a hint to prompt a correction of or addition to the previous answer. It invites the student to perform the appropriate action, given the information that it provides as an implicit negative assertion.

ST first responds to the RPQ with a *change of state token*, "o̲h." (line 60) (Heritage 1984a), after a .2 second pause. Heritage has called freestanding *oh* a *change-of-state token* because it is regularly used in conversation to show that the speaker has undergone a change in his or her "state of knowledge, information, orientation or awareness" (299). Two of the environments in which *oh* is used are relevant to this interaction: (1) in response to an *informing*, and (2) to display a *noticing*. If we see ST's "o̲h." as a typical response to an informing, he is responding to the RPQ, not as a question, but as an assertion which gives him new information. However, given the .2 second pause after the RPQ (line 59), it is more likely that ST's "o̲h." is not a direct response to an *informing* but is used to display a *noticing*. The RPQ sends him back to the text to look for an addition to his previous answer. After he finds this addition, he first displays that noticing with "o̲h." and then continues by redoing his previous answer.

ST redoes his answer by adding the remainder of the verb phrase to his original answer. By putting contrastive stress on the first word in the addition, he shows that it is a correction of the previous answer: "c̲ould have been saved."

(line 60). ST's response shows that he sees this question as prompting him to redo his answer, specifically to add to his previous answer. TJ's response to ST's self-correction, "there ya go." (line 61), by evaluating that self-correction as correct, also shows TJ's orientation to this question as a prompt to add to the previous answer.

This RPQ has many similarities to other-initiated repair done as a prompt for self-correction, discussed in Chapter 2. These other-initiated repairs, as described by Schegloff, Jefferson and Sacks (1977), are done as partial or full repeats of a prior turn with upward intonation and can result in self-correction, as in the following example:

(50) TG
```
01  Ava:        Well Monday, lemme think.
02              Monday, Wednesday an' Fridays I'm
03              home by one ten.
04  Bea:  -->   One ten?
05  Ava:  -->   Two o'clock. My class ends
06              one ten.
```

The RPQ, "just saved?", also contains a repeat of a prior utterance, done with upward intonation, to elicit self-correction. It differs from the examples of other-initiated repair discussed by Schegloff, Jefferson and Sacks (1977) in that it contains an additional item: *just*. It suggests that there is more to the answer than *just* "saved."

The next example, from a different teacher/student conference, is the second in a series of short sequences that the teacher, TT, has charactrized as doing "language work". In each of these sequences the teacher assists the student, SA, to self-correct language errors. Here is the original student text that they are working on (the text is, at the beginning of this excerpt, unmarked for errors):

(51) SA Text
```
There is hardly any other man in history can tell more
about what power and leadership really mean than that
of Adolf Hitler.
```

TT begins this portion of the conference by suggesting that she and SA read the portion of text aloud to check for problems. SA at first fails to identify any problems:

(52) TT/SA11/15/96
```
12  TT:         ((sniff)) mkay let's just read it
13              out loud.
```

```
14  SA:    ok.
15         (0.8) ((TT & SA both gaze at text;
16         SA leans in closer to text))
17  SA:    ((clears throat))
18  TT:    an see if you think there's any
19         problem.
20         (0.2)
21         ok? .h ((reading)) "there's hardly
22         any other man in history can tell
23         more about what (.) power and
24         leadership really mean than that of
25         Adolf Hitler."
26         (2.5) ((TT & SA gaze at text))
27  SA:    (h)
28  TT:    any problems there? ((TT glances
29         briefly at SA and back at text))
30  SA:    uh:: ((creaky voice))
31         (1.0) ((TT & SA gaze at text))
32         I dunno. (h)
33         (0.2)
```

The interaction continues with SA performing the first in a series of self-corrections. He eliminates the words "that of" after prompting from the teacher, i.e., "There is hardly any other man in history can tell more about what power and leadership really mean than that of Adolf Hitler."

The excerpt below, which includes an RPQ (lines 69–71), begins after this first self-correction.

(53) TT/SA11/15/96
```
56  TT:          okay,=an then
57               [here,
58               [[((TT points to text))
59               (0.5)
60               you've got one verb,
61               (1.0) ((TT & SA gaze at text))
62               there is, right?
63  SA:          um hum
64  TT:          an then you have another verb,
65               can tell,
66               (1.8) ((TT & SA gaze at text))
67  SA:          um:.
68               (1.0) ((TT & SA gaze at text))
69  TT: -->      can you have two verbs
70      -->      in a sentence with
71      -->      [no connecting [word?
```

```
72  SA:      [um              [((whispering))
73           [(                            )]
74  TT:      [°there's hardly any other] man in
75           history
76           (.)
77  SA:      who can tell.
78           [((SA moves pen toward text
79           [and begins to write))
80  TT:      [yeah::[:.
81  SA:             [°(yeah)
82  TT:      ta da:
83           [ok.] good.=um hum
84  SA:      [°( )]
85           [((SA: lateral headshake, smile))
86  TT:      see you found it, .h tell more
87           about what power and leadership
88           really mean than: adolf hitler.
```

As we saw in the earlier segment (lines 12–33), the teacher, TT, began by reading the targeted sentence aloud and asked the student to say if there were any problems, but he was not able to identify any. Subsequently, together, they identify one problem and correct it by eliminating "that of". Because TT begins this sequence with "ok,=an then here," (lines 56–57), displaying an orientation to a continuation of the same type of action at a different point in the same sentence, it should be clear to SA that what TT is pursuing here is a second grammar correction. And as the previous grammar correction sequence was done as a teacher-assisted self-correction, there could be an expectation that the remaining sequences will also be assisted self-corrections.

Perhaps because SA had previously failed to identify errors in this sentence on his own, the teacher now offers the first hint for locating and correcting this second error: the error has something to do with the two verbs. She begins by pointing to SA's text while directing his orientation verbally to two verbs in the first clause: "is" and "can tell" (lines 60–65). There is a pause of 1.8 seconds (line 66) during which the student, if he has seen an error, could make the correction, but he does not.

The information that SA has so far is that the error has something to do with the two verbs. Yet there is no problem with the two verbs themselves. TT's next question, an RPQ, gives ST more information about what type of problem he should be looking for: "can you have two verbs in a sentence with no connecting word?" (lines 69–71). The teacher here is obviously not asking the student for information about English grammar; this is a *known-information* question. She is also not teaching a grammar rule through elicitation. In the environment of error correction, this question suggests that she is reminding the student of a grammar rule which both of them already know, i.e., that you cannot have two verbs in a sentence with no connecting word. This question is very similar to the other pedagogical RPQs in that, in this sequential context, the question is only interpretable as implying a negative assertion; this is the only way in which the course of action begun in this sequence can be furthered by this question. As in the previous pedagogical RPQ sequences, the teacher seems to be using this question to point to the reason why the student's text is grammatically inaccurate, and, at the same time, to give him a further hint how to self-correct the error, solving the problem posed earlier in Excerpt 52, lines 12–19.

As in Excerpt 49, the student does not respond to the question format or the implied criticism with a *no* answer. Rather, he responds to the action that it invites him to perform, given the information that it provides as a hint. However, there is a problem with this hint. It does not accurately diagnose the problem and, in consequence, does not imply a correct solution. The problem here is not the lack of a connecting word between two verbs in one sentence, or clause, with the same subject, but lack of a relative pronoun/subject for the second verb. This may be why the hint does not produce an immediate correction. SA seems to understand that the question is asking for an action: a correction. He orients to this action by continuing to display attention to the problematic portion of the text, whispering the text to himself as if searching for a solution to the error (lines 72–73).

Perhaps as a result of SA's continued demonstrated inability to perform the elicited action, TT adds an additional prompt, which I have called a *designedly incomplete utterance* (Koshik 2002b). She reads the portion of text up to the possible correction and stops, prompting SA to complete the rest of the sentence with the correction, which he does:

```
74  TT:    [°there's hardly any other] man in
75         history
76         (.)
77  SA:    who can tell.
```

SA's stress on the word "who" shows that this is the element he is adding as a correction.

As SA writes the correction in the text, the teacher agrees with his answer (line 80), celebrates his achievement (line 82), and positively evaluates his answer (line 83). She finishes this correction sequence by reading the corrected version after giving the student additional praise (lines 86–88):

```
77 SA:   who can tell.
78       [((SA moves pen toward text
79       [and begins to write))
80 TT:   [yeah::[:.
81 SA:          [°(yeah)
82 TT:   ta da:
83       [ok. ] good.=um hum
84 SA:   [°( )]
85       [((SA: lateral headshake, smile))
86 TT:   see you found it, .h tell more
87       about what power and leadership
88       really mean than: adolf hitler.
```

In summary, in Excerpts 49 and 53 the two teachers use RPQs to perform an action similar to that of the RPQs discussed earlier in this chapter: they show what is problematic about either the student's text or the student's talk and suggest a solution. But this action is used to perform a second action: to assist student performance already in progress when the student demonstrates an inability to perform correctly. These RPQs, like the previous RPQs, convey a negative assertion, but their preference structure is complicated by their use in assisting on-going student performance, making a course of action relevant as a response. Because the RPQs are used as hints to enable a student to produce a correct second pair part and accomplish a previously-invited action, the questions do not elicit answers but the action which a *no* answer would make relevant. The previous RPQ sequences were pursuing clarification of a problem and a potential solution to be implemented sometime after the conference. In the grammar correction sequences, the solution is to be implemented now, during the conference, and it is the accomplishment of this solution that is treated as the preferred response to the RPQ. In cases of multiple preference where the two preferences are not congruent but are cross-cutting with differing preference structures, it is the preference structure of the action, rather than the vehicle for the action, that dominates (Schegloff 1995b, to appear). It may be that the preference structure of the action dominates even in some cases where the preferences are congruent, especially where a preferred answer to the question assists the recipient to perform an ongoing action. This may be more likely in the case of RPQs where the preferred answer to the question has already been implied.

These RPQ sequences also have implications for sequence structure. The original request to make the correction seems to retain its force as a first pair part, even when an answer is provided, if that answer is inadequate; the sequence is not closed until a correct second pair part is articulated (cf. Mehan 1985). Further research may show this to be a general characteristic of pedagogical known-information question sequences.

The RPQs in Excerpts 49 and 53 also differ from those discussed earlier in this chapter in their centrality to the sequence in which they are used. In the content and organization sequences, the RPQs are central to the action that the sequence is accomplishing, even in the one example where the RPQ is used contingently to refer to prior student talk. The sequences in which they are used are initiated by targeting a problematic portion of student text. The RPQs perform a central role in those sequences by showing what is problematic about that portion of text and suggesting a solution to be implemented outside the conference. In the grammar correction sequences, the RPQs are used contingently as hints only when students evidence difficulty in accomplishing the elicited action. In the interaction where the student was asked to name verb phrases, his answer was incomplete and the RPQ was used to hint that the answer needed expanding. In the second interaction, the student evidenced trouble finding and correcting the grammar error in the targeted sentence. The RPQ was used as a hint to help him find and correct the error. The use of the RPQ was, in both examples, contingent on the student displaying that he needed help to perform an on-going action correctly.

CHAPTER 5

Alternative question error correction sequences

In the previous chapter we saw how the sequences of action in which RPQs are used can be designed to accomplish pedagogically-specific goals. We can call these *practices of pedagogical talk,* rather than ordinary conversational practices which happen to be used in a pedagogical setting. This chapter continues the focus on pedagogical practices by discussing a type of alternative question used by teachers (or parents "doing teaching" with their children) to prompt learners to self-correct their errors, either oral or written. As we will see, these alternative questions are closely related to the RPQs discussed in Chapters 2 and 4 in that the first alternative functions like a yes/no RPQ.

In order to explain the functions of pedagogical alternative question error corrections, it will first be necessary to provide some background on conversational repair practices and the actions, or functions, they perform. After introducing conversational repair practices, I describe the unique role that alternative questions play as repair initiators. I contrast alternative question repair initiators that seek to clarify alternate hearings or understandings with those that target errors and present candidate corrections. Alternative questions that seek to clarify alternate hearings or understandings correspond to the "real", information-seeking questions discussed in earlier chapters. Those that present candidate corrections incorporate *reversed polarity questions* that display the epistemic stance of the speaker.

After contrasting these two different functions, I focus in more detail on alternative questions used to elicit error correction in pedagogical interactions. Those that initiate error correction on student talk resemble conversational repair initiators in the way they interrupt an ongoing sequence of talk to deal with a problem, although they are used almost exclusively in pedagogical interactions. I also discuss an extension of this practice, used to initiate error correction on student writing. I conclude with a discussion on how recipients recognize the different actions preformed by alternative question repair initiators.

5.1 Other-initiated (OI) repair

The conversation analytic literature on the organization of repair (e.g., Egbert 1996, 1997; Hosoda 2000, 2001; Jefferson 1974, 1987; Kim 1999, 2001; Koshik 2005; Schegloff 1979, 1987b, 1992, 1997a, 1997b, 2000; Schegloff et al. 1977; Wong 2000) describes practices for interrupting the ongoing course of action to deal with problems in speaking, hearing, and/or understanding the talk (Schegloff 1995b, 1997a; Schegloff et al. 2002). When describing these practices, conversation analysts distinguish between repair initiation and its outcome. Repair can be initiated by the speaker of the *trouble source*, or talk being repaired (i.e., *self-initiated repair*). Alternatively, repair can be initiated by someone other than the speaker of the trouble source, i.e., *other-initiated*, or *OI*, repair. Similarly, either self- or other-initiated repair can be brought to completion by the speaker of the trouble source or its recipient.

When someone else initiates repair on a prior speaker's utterance, i.e., OI repair, that repair initiation targets the trouble source more or less specifically. Among the practices for targeting the trouble source are repair initiators such as "huh?" or "what?" ; phrases such as "whaddyou mean"; wh-question words such as "who", "where" and "when", used alone or together with a partial repeat of the trouble source turn, i.e., "met whom?"; the phrase "y' mean" plus an candidate understanding of the prior talk; and a partial or full repeat of the prior talk with upward intonation (Schegloff 1997a; Schegloff et al. 1977). "Open class" (Drew 1997) repair initiators such as "huh?" target the trouble source least specifically, and display the weakest grasp of the targeted utterance. Partial or full repetitions of the prior utterance, on the other hand, display the strongest grasp of the trouble source and target it most specifically (Schegloff 1997a).

5.2 Actions performed by OI repairs that repeat the trouble source

OI repairs regularly initiate a sequence of at least two turns, the repair initiation and the response by the speaker of the trouble source. Repair initiations formed by repeating the trouble source can be used to do a number of different actions, and the response varies depending on the action that the repair is heard to be performing.

5.2.1 Presenting candidate hearings for confirmation

Perhaps the most common action is to present a candidate hearing of the trouble source for confirmation. In this case, the response is either a confirmation or a correction of the proffered hearing.

Hearing confirmed
The following excerpt, from (Schegloff 1997a), exemplifies a confirmation (line 12) of the candidate hearing (line 11).

```
(54)  NB, 1-2-1
      01 Guy:        What's-w-'what kind of a
      02             starting time ken:: we get
      03             fer:: hh sometime this
      04             afternoon.
      05             (0.7)
      06             Any[time-
      07 Clk:           [Oh:::, [let's see.
      08 Guy:                   [Anytime tuhday.
      09 Clk:        Two fordy.
      10 Clk:        One, thirdy.
      11 Guy:  -->   One thirty?
      12 Clk:  -->   Mm hm::?
      13 Guy:        One thirty.
      14             (1.0)
      15 Guy:        .hh W'l at sounds like a good
      16             time?
```

Mishearing corrected
The candidate hearing can also turn out to be a mishearing, however, and be corrected in the next turn, as in the following excerpt, also from (Schegloff 1997a):

```
(55)  IND PD 59
      01 Police:     Radio,
      02 Caller:     One six nine South Hampton
      03             Road, on the east side,
      04 Police:     What's the trouble lady,
      05 Caller:     I don't know my husband's
      06             sitting in his chair I don't
      07             know what's wrong with him
      08             he can't talk or move or
      09             anything.
```

```
10 Police:   --> Four six nine South Hampton?
11 Caller:   --> One six nine South Hampton.
```

5.2.2 Displaying lack of understanding and eliciting an explanation

Another action that can be performed with this repair practice is displaying lack of understanding and eliciting an explanation. Although there is a turn design specifically devoted to this action, i.e., "whaddyou mean", used by itself or followed by a repetition of the trouble source,[35] this action can also be performed by a repetition alone. Using a repetition of the trouble source to express trouble understanding a prior utterance may be more common in talk with those who are not yet proficient in the language, as in the following example. The excerpt is taken from a conversation in a women's locker room after a practice session by several members of a university women's hockey team.[36] Eriko is a native speaker of Japanese who has recently arrived in the U.S and still has limited English proficiency. The other participants are native speakers of American English. After receiving an invitation to play pond hockey with the others, Eriko initiates several repairs to elicit help understanding the invitation turn and subsequent attempts by the co-participants to explain that invitation turn.

(56) **Pond Hockey**
```
01 Jan:          Eriko (.) do you wanna play
02               u:m pond hockey tomorrow?
03               (0.2)
04 Eriko:  -->   ↑(hockey)↑
05               (0.4)
06 Jan:          pond hockey?
07 Eriko:  -->   pond hockey?
08 Jan:          yeah:.
09 Geri:         outside
10 Jan:          [outside]
11 Geri:         [at my  ]mom's house.
12               (0.6)
13 Eriko:  -->   mom?
14 Geri:         my m:om's house.
15               (0.3)
16 Jan:          her (.) her mother's.
17               (1.0)
18 Geri:         we're gunna (.) play hockey=
19 Jan:          =do you want to? outside?
20 Eriko:        ye:ah.
```

Eriko's first repair initiation consists of a repetition of an element in the invitation, a term that she was already familiar with, "↑hockey↑" (line 4). This may be either a candidate hearing or an attempt to elicit further explanation of the invitation. Jan treats the repair as a candidate hearing, repeating the complete phrase, "pond hockey?" (line 6). This may be a slight correction, adding the missing portion of the noun phrase. She does this repeat with upward intonation, as if reissuing the invitation. Eriko initiates repair again (line 7), repeating Jan's entire prior turn and stressing the unfamiliar term, "pond hockey?". Jan again interprets this as a candidate hearing and simply confirms it (line 8). Geri, however, seems to understand that Eriko is displaying trouble understanding the term *pond hockey*. She offers an explanation, "outside" (line 9), which Jan repeats (line 10). However, when Geri continues by adding additional information, "at my mom's house." (line 11), she also unfortunately adds to the confusion. Although the word *mom* is common among native speakers of American English, it is not a high-frequency vocabulary word in many English as a foreign language textbooks. Eriko again initiates repair by repeating the problem word, "mom?" (line 13). This time, Geri is the one who hears the repair initiation as a candidate hearing, and both confirms and expands it (line 14) by repeating the full noun phrase from her prior utterance. Jan, however, appears to realize that Eriko is eliciting help understanding the term. Jan offers an explanation by substituting a higher frequency vocabulary word, "mother" (line 16). By this time, however, even if Eriko has understood some of the individual words, there is no evidence that she has understood the action being proffered, i.e., that it is an invitation, as she still does not respond to the invitation (line 17). After the invitation is collaboratively reissued, using higher frequency vocabulary and decomposed into simpler syntactic constructions (lines 18–19), Eriko finally displays understanding by accepting it (line 20).

In this excerpt, we have seen that partial or full repetitions of a prior utterance can be used to display trouble understanding and to elicit an explanation.[37] However, we have also seen that the different actions being performed by repetitions of a trouble source are not always unequivocally understood by recipients.[38] I will return to this observation later in Chapter 6.

5.2.3 Prompting for self-correction: Pre-disagreement

Finally, as discussed in Chapter 2, under certain circumstances, repetitions can be heard as targeting a trouble source in the prior utterance for the recipient to self-correct, especially when contrastive stress is added to the targeted error, as in the following example from Schegloff et al. (1977):

(57) GTS:3:42
```
01 A:      Hey the first time they stopped
02         me from sellin cigarettes was
03         this morning.
04         (1.0)
05 B: -->  From selling cigarettes?
06 A: -->  From buying cigarettes.
```

As shown earlier, this hearing is more likely when the person initiating the repair has epistemic authority, i.e., an equal or greater claim to knowledge about the trouble source (cf. Heritage & Raymond in preparation; Koshik 2002a, 2003), or if an error in the targeted talk is self-evident. We saw in the discussion of Excerpt 17, Chapter 2, how teachers make use of this repair initiation to target student errors for self-correction. An ESL teacher targeted a lexical error in a student's answer by repeating it with exaggerated upward intonation and stress: "daughters:". The student subsequently corrected the error to "father."

We will turn now to OI repairs initiated by alternative questions to see what using this form accomplishes that the more common simple repetition does not.

5.3 Actions performed by alternative question repairs

Alternative questions have a specific intonation pattern that differentiates them from yes/no questions. According to Quirk and Greenbaum (1973:198), the alternative question "contains a separate nucleus for each alternative: a rise occurs on each item in the list, except the last, on which there is a fall, indicating that the list is complete". They provide the following constructed example to distinguish alternative questions from yes/no questions:[39]

(58) **Quirk and Greenbaum (1973:198)**
alternative: A: Shall we go by BÚS or TRÀIN? B: By BÙS.
yes/no: A: Shall we go by bus or TRÁIN? B: No, let's take the CÀR.

Unlike yes/no questions, that invite a *yes* or *no* answer, alternative questions invite as an answer one of the two alternatives presented in the question.

OI repairs that use alternative questions are very rare, so rare that they have not until very recently been discussed in the repair literature (Koshik 2005). When speakers do use alternative questions to initiate repair, rather than one of the more common repair initiators, what does using this form accomplish that the other forms discussed above do not?

5.3.1 Clarifying alternate hearings

Like the repetitions of the trouble source in Excerpts 54 and 55, alternative questions can also be used to present candidate hearings, but the design of an alternative question enables speakers to present two possible alternate hearings of an item in a prior utterance. Here are some examples. The first is from a discussion among teenage boys.

```
(59)   GTS 4, 28
       01 Ken:       Bu-that convertible we went to
       02            Huntington Beach an' he jumped.
       03            He jumped outta the convertible
       04            goin sixty miles an hour.
       05            [Big fat slob-
       06 Rog: -->   [Six<u>teen</u> or sixty.
       07 Ken:       We-I-di-wu-we were on the f-on
       08            that Huntington Coast Road?
```

In this example, the form of an alternative question is used to present two candidate hearings which sound similar and could possibly be confused, especially since the alternate hearing, "sixteen", is more likely in this context. The repair is formed by simply presenting the two possible hearings, contrasting them using "or". The order of the two alternatives does not appear to be interactionally significant. Like other alternative questions with two choices, there is a rise on the first alternative (here shown by the additional stress which, in American English includes a rise in pitch), and downward final intonation on the second. Roger stresses the final syllable of "six<u>teen</u>", possibly to clearly distinguish it phonologically from the other hearing, "sixty". The first syllables of the two words are identical, except for their stress, and the final syllables are phonologically similar. Ken does not respond to the repair initiation, possibly because it is done in overlap with his own talk.

In the next example, the speaker who is initiating repair in lines 32–33 is also offering two alternate hearings. This excerpt is from an official phone call from a hospital to a fire department. The caller is requesting transportation to the airport for a female stretcher patient now at the hospital.

```
(60)   FD IV, 2-3
       01 D:      seven twunny four, fire
       02         department emergency,
       03 S:      yeah, This Is missis baxster.
       04         at the presbyterian hospital.
       05         n' I have a patient that I would
```

```
06            like tuh ree- red wagon. hh to
07            transfer out to innernational
08            airport.
09  D:        what time.
10  S:        and the patient, uh is expected
11            by P.N.A., an' she's to be there
12            no later than ten fifteen. so
13            that they can uh load her first.
14            and she is a stretcher patient.
15  D:        'ka::y, now: ( ) she be there by
16            ten fifteen a.m. this morning.
17            right?
18  S:        uh huh,
19  D:        o-ka:y, uh, where's this plane uh
20            in route to.
21  S:        uh::, seattle.
22  D:        seattle? 'ka:y, mhh
23            presbyterian, where do they
24            pick 'er up, third floor at
25            presbyterian,
26  S:        y:eah.
27            ((pause))
28  D:        wha' was yer first name please,
29  S:        mi:ne? kathrine.
30  D:        kathrine, (scottwick.)
31            ((pause))
32  S: -->    my first name? 'r her
33            first[name.
34  D:            [yers.
35  S:        yah::, ka:thrine, hhh
36  D:        o:ka::[y,
37  S:              [hheh
```

The caller self-identifies (lines 3–4) with title and last name, "Missis Baxster", and institutional affiliation. After she gives her request (lines 5–8) and the dispatcher establishes the time and location for pickup and the ultimate destination of the patient (lines 9–26), the dispatcher asks for the caller's first name: "Wha' was yer first name please," (line 28). When said with normal phonological reduction, the pronouns "your" and "her" can sound almost indistinguishable. Compare, for example, "yer" in line 28 with "'er" in line 24, referring to the patient. The caller initiates repair on the dispatcher's question, repeating the person reference, with change of deixis, "Mi:ne?" (line 29), and then, without waiting for an answer, goes on to give her first name. The dispatcher then repeats the name (line 30), adding an additional unclear utterance, one that could possibly be heard as a last name, but not the one given by the caller in line 3. Perhaps because of uncertainty induced by a possible last name not her own, the caller again initiates repair on the original question, this time using an alternative question that contrasts the two possible hearings (lines 32–33). The two alternatives are made up of two noun phrases, with the two alternate hearings (with change of deictic reference) given contrastive stress. The full noun phrase is used perhaps because the repair is not being initiated on the immediately prior turn. The contrastive stress highlights the problematic person reference. The dispatcher responds by repeating one of the person references, again with change of deixis (line 34).

The following more complex excerpt[40] shows a slight variation on this practice. This excerpt is taken from a car trip to an extended family party. The participants in this excerpt are the mother, Ann (in her 50's), father Dick, son Fred, daughter Deb, and Deb's husband Marty. Prior to this excerpt, Ann and Deb had been having a partially mock argument initiated by Deb's complaint, "How come I never got a trousseau." In an attempt to diffuse the argument, Dick had responded with a pun, "Because you had a falso." This excerpt begins with Dick's praise of his earlier pun, addressed to his son-in-law, Marty. Dick's self-praise gets rejected by both his daughter and his wife. Marty then comes to his aid with an aphorism (lines 13–14), interspersed with laughter, that both compliments Dick and teasingly criticizes his wife and daughter's disapproving remarks. Dick twice initiates repair on Marty's compliment, the second time with an alternative question (lines 48–51). Because this repair initiation targets a trouble source that is not in the immediately preceding talk, the trouble source and its repetition are highlighted with a single-headed arrow, and the alternative question repair with a double-headed arrow.

```
(61)   PreParty:12
       01 Dick:      ((falsetto)) (Mar-) Marty I
       02            like(d) that quote. It wasn' a
       03            trousseau it was a falso.
       04 Deb:       Oh:[:
       05 Dick:         [I like(d) tha' one.
       06 Deb:       fa:ther.=
       07 Mart:      =[Y i h d o :, ]
       08 Ann:       =[Well yer the o]nly one that
       09            likes it.
       10 Mart:      °Ahh
       11 Dick:      Alright.
       12            (4.2)
       13 Mart:  --> Fi(h)ne sensibilities are
```

```
14                  never wi:despread.
15                  (0.4)
16   Deb:           ehh!
17   Fred:          Mhh=
18   Ann:           =[Wha::t.
19   Fred:          =[hmm hmm,
20   Deb:           hah [hah hah hah, huh,]
21   Dick:              [Uh repeat that,   ]
22   Deb:           ah-h-h ah-h-h
23                  (1.5)
24   Dick:          I:, missed it.
25                  (0.4)
26   Deb:           He's talking for posterity.
27   Mart:          No:,
28                  (0.4)
29   Deb:           hhh
30   Mart:          'a wz a:, perfectly good
31                  commend=yer father said he
32                  liked it 'n nobody else liked
33                  it so I said.
34          -->    .hh Fine sensibilities are not
35                  widespread.
36   Deb:           [°Hmm,
37   Dick?:         [Aaww::
38                  (0.9)
39                  Tha'ss very good.
40                  (.)
41                  I appreciate (it).
42   Fred:          A joke with en escape hatch.
43                  (I) [gotta remember dat.
44                  Hu:h.
45   Mart:          [((clears throat))
46                  (5.0)
47   Deb:           [Uh,
48   Dick:  -->>   [Did he say, The- thing I
49                  don't understdidju
50          -->>   say wi:despread or
51                  whitespread.
52   Mart:          °Oh:[:
53   Deb:               [Oh:[::
54   Mart:                  [°no.
55   Deb:           f-father hh
56   Deb:           How [come you get this,
57   Anne:              [Will you please
58                  concen[trate on driving the=
```

```
59  Deb:            [t hi s v::ve r s i o n
60                  o[f jovial.
61  Anne:           car.=
62  Dick:           =[ I:'m stuck.
```

Dick twice initiates repair on Marty's compliment. The first time, he requests a repeat (line 21), claiming trouble hearing it (line 24). After Marty repeats his compliment (lines 34–35), Dick responds with a positive assessment (line 39) and a statement of appreciation (line 41), demonstrating that he has heard and understood Marty's compliment. Some time later, however, Dick initiates repair once again on the same compliment. This repair initiation, done as a joke, begins with an explicit marking of the repair as trouble hearing/understanding (lines 48–49), followed by an alternative question which presents two mock alternate hearings of the final item in Marty's compliment (lines 49–51). The use of an alternative question here gives Dick the chance to make another pun, which is subsequently rejected by the other participants. This alternative question, unlike those in the prior two examples, does not begin with a repeat of the trouble source, but is embedded in a frame that makes its action, however mock, explicit.

We have just seen how the form of an alternative question can be used to present two possible phonologically similar hearings of an item in a prior utterance. The use of an alternative question rather than a yes/no question allows the repair initiator to contrast two similar hearings, specifying that the problem is one of hearing the difference between them. The form of an alternative question makes relevant a response that repeats the trouble source, ratifying one of the two alternatives. If the repair initiator simply presented one possible hearing, a *yes* response to this hearing might not clarify the ambiguity, especially if the recipient does not understand that the problem is one of distinguishing between two possible hearings.

5.3.2 Clarifying alternate understandings

A second, related reason for using an alternative question in OI repair is to contrast two different items that have been confused in the prior talk, in order to clarify which was meant. The following excerpt is taken from an informal one-on-one tutoring session between a native and a non-native speaker of English.[41] The non-native speaker of English (SJ), an international graduate student from Korea, has hired the native speaker (TJ), a former graduate student who has been trained to teach English as a Second Language, to help him improve his conversational English. Excerpt 62 is taken from the portion of the session during which the two are engaged in mundane conversation. SJ has been talking about one of his classes in which he has to give a presentation. He is complaining about the professor's insistence that each student speak in class. SJ says that the professor is confusing this class, in his major field, with an English (i.e., English as a second language) class. According to SJ, the professor is emphasizing English skills for the non-native speakers in the class because the professor is from India and has evidently had trouble, himself, learning English as a second language. The excerpt begins with the first mention of the professor of this class. TJ's repair initiation (line 30) targets SJ's confusion of "he" and "she".

(62)   TJ & SJ / 2002
```
01 SJ:      so: (0.2) there are- there are
02          um: loose time. I gue- (0.5)
03          .hhh but (.) the professor (0.2)
04          want .hh uh:: at- each student
05          spea:k.
06 TJ:      mm hm.
07 SJ:      .hh (never) understand it's not
08          English class. .hh (°eh:, so)
09          she's- she- um confused English
10          class [en
11 TJ:            [hm heh heh heh [heh
12 SJ:                            [mas- uh::
13          the major class.
14 TJ:      uh huh.=
15 SJ:      =yeah.
16          (0.2)
17 SJ:      she: uh=he is (.) Indian. t! his
18          English (0.2) >is not< goo:d.
19          heh heh heh so: .h uh:: I guess
20          she: uh he um::: t! I g- he
21          ha:ve experience the:: Eng-
22          uh:: troublem- troubles in
23          English so: .hh she emphasi:ze
24          [(to-) en
25 TJ:      [mm hm
26          English I guess um tch!
27 SJ:      .hh hh °e:h [e:n
28 TJ:                  [yeah.
29 SJ:      she:: but=
30 TJ: -->  =he?=or she.
31 SJ:      oh he:.
32 TJ:      uh huh.
```

As is evident in lines 9, 17, 20, 23, and 29, SJ is having problems with the third person singular pronoun, confusing the genders. This is a common problem among English learners whose first language does not normally make use of third person singular pronouns in spoken communication.

After his first mention of the professor in line 3, he subsequently refers to him as "she" (lines 9 and 17), corrects the pronoun to "he" and refers to "his" English in line 17, then refers to him as "she" in line 20, correcting to "he" in the same line, and twice later refers to him as "she" (lines 23 and 29). TJ, who does not know this professor, finally interrupts (line 30) with a repair initiation in the form of an alternative question.

Although TJ might suspect that the professor is male, given the direction of most of SJ's corrections, i.e., from *she* to *he*, he has no way of knowing this for sure. This repair initiation cannot therefore be considered a correction. It does, however, elicit a correction. It does this by making use of the same form as that of the repair initiation in Excerpt 59. But unlike the repair initiation in Excerpt 59, the two items contrasted here are not two possible hearings, but two alternate forms, both of which occurred in the prior talk. This repair initiation elicits a correction by eliciting a clarification of which of the two alternative forms was intended. As in the prior examples, the order of the two alternatives does not seem to be interactionally significant. It seems rather to be influenced by the order in which these two items are normally collocated in English.

Why use an alternative question here rather than a more common repair initiation? If TJ had used the more common initiation, a repetition of the trouble source with upward intonation, i.e., "she?", the source of the problem might not be made clear. A repetition of the trouble source could be misunderstood as a candidate hearing proffered for confirmation (cf. Excerpt 54), in which case the response could have merely been a confirming "yes". Alternatively, this kind of repair could be heard as targeting a trouble source for self-correction (cf. Excerpt 57); however, in this case the tutor would have been conveying a stance that the feminine pronoun was problematic, and at this point he did not know for sure which was the correct gender. By using an alternative question, he can therefore make the source of the problem clear by contrast. The fact that SJ's first response to the repair initation was "oh" (line 31), shows that this repair initiation has given him new information (Heritage 1984a). It seems to have brought to his conscious attention his confusion between the two forms and the trouble it was causing for the other participant. TJ's job is to help SJ improve his English. TJ's use of an alternative question here can facilitate SJ's language acquisiton by focusing SJ's attention on his confusion of the two forms, and eliciting a repetition of the correct alternative.

5.3.3 Targeting errors and presenting candidate corrections

As we have seen, the use of alternative questions to present two alternate candidate hearings or understandings allows the repair initiator to specify more explicitly the nature of the problem. We have also seen that when alternative question repairs are initiated for these purposes, the person who is initiating repair does not convey a preference for one of the two alternatives over the other. The order in which they are given does not appear to be interactionally significant. This agrees with Bolinger (1957:119), who makes a strong claim that the majority of alternative questions do not exhibit a particular preference for one alternative over the other:

> The various suasive modifications of yes-no Qs – negative conduciveness, imputations, tentations, and pyramiding – are of limited use in alQs [i.e., alternative questions], partly because of structure (the complications caused by adding something more to a Q already more intricate than most yes-no), but mostly because of meaning. The majority of alQs convey two or more choices that are equally plausible; if the speaker had strong reasons for rejecting one of them, he would be more likely not to mention it at all.

However, alternative question repair initiations *can* exhibit a preference for one alternative over the other. This occurs when they are used to do, and are heard to be doing, error correction, i.e., proffering one alternative, the second one, as a candidate correction of an utterance targeted in the first alternative. The previously-described use of alternative questions to present alternative candidate hearings or understandings is very rare. The practice of using alternative questions to do error correction is even more rare in ordinary conversation, although it is quite common in pedagogical interactions. The following excerpt is the only one that I have (except in a joke sequence, to be discussed later) that is not said by an expert, i.e., teacher or parent, to a learner. Although the talk occurs in a pedagogical setting, the speakers are both students. The data segment is taken from a graduate seminar discussion on English for Specific Purposes[42] classes and their value for language students who are professionals in the field being targeted.[43] Libby, the speaker of the trouble source, is discussing research on the intelligibility of simplified technical manuals for both professionals and non-professionals in the field. This information is from an article that she has read but the other students did not have access to. When Tamar initiates repair on a word in Libby's prior talk, using an alternative question (line 6), Libby demonstrates that she hears the second alternative as a correction, which she rejects.

(63) **Waring: Graduate Seminar**
```
01 Lib:      .hhh and in fact (0.2) the ones
02           who had no specialization
03           (0.8).h understood (.) the
04           revi:sed manual better and
05           could explain it.=
06 Tam:  --> =revised 'r abridged.
07 Lib:      u- well it was re[vised, it]
08 Tam?:                      [(       )]
09 Lib:      wasn't abridged.=cause [they
10 Tam?:                            [(    )
11 Lib:      didn't shorten it. they- they
12           re:wrote it. [totally.
13 (?):                   [uh huh
14 Lib:      .h but the ones who were
15           specialized, who knew how
16           missiles worked,
17 Tam:      Mm hum.
18 Lib:      said (0.2) there's something
19           wrong here. it's not following
20           the genre.
```

In line 6 Tamar initiates repair on a word in Libby's prior utterance, using an alternative question. Although the form of the question is very similar to the alternative question repairs in Excerpts 59 and 62, the action that the question is heard to be doing is different. The first alternative, "revised", targets the trouble source in the prior utterance by repeating it.[44] The second alternative, "abridged", provides an alternative to that trouble source. The order of the two alternatives is therefore significant.

Unlike the second alternative in Excerpts 59–61, "abridged" cannot be heard as an alternate hearing; it is not phonologically similar to "revised." Neither was it provided by the speaker of the prior talk as in Excerpt 62, where the repair seeks to clarify which of the two choices was meant. It is an item in the same class as the targeted trouble source, presented as a candidate alternative to the trouble source by the person initiating the repair. By offering an alternative to a term used by the recipient, one that cannot be understood as an alternate hearing, it suggests that the original term be reconsidered in favor of the alternative. This second alternative is, however, presented as a *candidate* correction, not a full correction, because it is presented as one of two choices; it is still up to the speaker of the trouble source to choose the second alternative.

What is the evidence that Libby hears this as a correction? In a turn designed as a dispreferred utterance (the turn is delayed by "u-" and "well"), showing Libby's orientation to this as a disagreement with Tamar, Libby first reaffirms the correctness of the term Tamar had targeted as in error: "it was re̱vised," (line 7), and then she explicitly rejects the candidate correction: "it wa̱sn't abridged." (lines 7, 9). The contrastive stress on "re̱vised" emphasizes this as the correct term, and the contrastive stress on "wa̱sn't" shows that Libby has understood Tamar to be proposing the term, "abridged," as the correct one. Libby then goes on to give an account for her reaffirmation of the word "revised": "=cause they didn't shorten it. they- they re:wrote it. to̱tally." (lines 9, 11–12). This account also displays Libby's orientation to her turn as a disagreement.

Following this short repair sequence, Libby continues with the sequence that had been interrupted by the repair. The "but" which begins her utterance in line 14, after her in-breath, links this utterance back to lines 1–5 prior to Tamar's repair initiation. In lines 1–5 Libby had been discussing the reaction of the non-professionals to the simplified manuals. In lines 14–16 and 18–20 she contrasts the non-professional reaction with that of the professionals. The main sequence that had been interrupted by the repair sequence is thus resumed.

In this use of an alternative question repair, both the design of the first alternative and the practice it is used to accomplish resemble partial repeats of a prior utterance used to target a trouble source in order to elicit self-correction or backdown, as in Excerpt 57. It is therefore a *yes/no RPQ* that displays the stance of the speaker, i.e., that the portion of the prior utterance repeated in the first alternative is problematic. In Excerpt 63, Tamar conveys a stance that the correct word to describe the manual is *not* "revised".

The second alternative resembles another type of conversational repair initiation that has not yet been discussed. As we have seen, not all repair, as defined by conversation analysts, accomplishes error correction.[45] Often, repair initiations are done to present candidate hearings or understandings and the understanding is simply confirmed, as in Excerpt 54. Even when repair is initiated on someone else's prior talk in order to have an error corrected, the person initiating repair often merely targets the problematic portion of the utterance and leaves it up to the original speaker to correct in the next turn, as in Excerpt 57. However, speakers can also initiate repair on a prior speaker's utterance by providing a candidate correction. This candidate correction targets a trouble source inexplicitly by providing a substitute of the same class, leaving it for the speaker of the trouble to merely accept or reject the candidate correction. Examples of *other-initiated, other-completed repair* in the literature have, until now, consisted of this type of practice. Here is an example from Schegloff et al. (1977: 378):

```
(64)  JS:11:97
      01  Lori:       But y'know single beds'r awfully
      02              thin tuh sleep on.
      03  Sam:        What?
      04  Lori:       Single beds. [They're-
      05  Ellen: -->               [Y' mean narrow?
      06  Lori:       they're awfully narrow [yeah,
```

Here Ellen (line 5) does not explicitly target the trouble source by repeating it, but rather targets it inexplicitly by offering another lexical item of the same category, "narrow," as a substitute for, and thus a candidate correction of, "thin." She does this as a question, eliciting an acceptance of the candidate correction from Lori (line 6).

Alternative questions that target errors and present candidate corrections thus resemble two different repair initiation practices, one that targets a trouble source by repeating it, and one that provides a candidate correction. Because the first alternative is questioned, by means of an RPQ, the second alternative is heard as the preferred alternative. Therefore, if the speaker of the trouble source rejects the correction, this rejection can take on the character of a disagreement, as was seen in Excerpt 63.

5.3.4 Alternative question error corrections as vehicles for other actions

Participants can use alternative question error corrections as a vehicle for other actions. The following excerpt (taken from Schegloff 1984) is from a radio call-in show. A is the radio personality and B is the caller. According to Schegloff, B has been describing to A "the differences he (B) has been having with his high school history teacher over the morality of American foreign policy since the time of George Washington" (28, 29).

```
(65)
      01  B:    Because- an'he did the same
      02        thing, in War of- the War of
      03        Eighteen Twelve, he said the fact
      04        that we were interested in
      05        expansion, t' carrying farther,
      06        was () something against. Y'know
      07        a-argument t'use against. But
      08        see the whole thing is he's
```

```
09              against, he's
10              [very- he's ()
11 A: -->       [Is he teaching history or
12    -->       divinity
13 B:           I don'kno(h)w. But he's very
14              anti-imperialistic.
```

Schegloff uses this excerpt to exemplify sequences which are packaged in a question-answer format but which are not used to ask or answer a question. According to Schegloff, the question in lines 11–12 is not a question about subject matter and the response in line 13 is not a confession of ignorance. Earlier in the conversation, the following talk occurs, which makes it clear that the class in question is a history class:

(66)
```
B: ... I'm taking 'merican history this
   term, I'm a junior. Well I- now the
   new term began I gotta new teacher, so,
   we're starting from about you know,
   Washington's foreign policy
   ((interpolations by A omitted in the
   original))
```

If we extend Schegloff's analysis, we can see why this sequence is not asking or answering an information-seeking question. First of all, the question is formatted as an alternative question repair. The first alternative ostensibly targets the prior assertion that the teacher was a history teacher, and the second alternative suggests a "correction." However, it is in fact a mock error correction, conveying the ironic suggestion that the teacher seems to be teaching divinity rather than history. In thus challenging the teacher, the radio host displays alignment with the caller's criticism of the teacher. The radio host's ability to use this utterance to display alignment with the caller is predicated on the caller's understanding of the question as a (mock) other-initiated error correction. The caller's "I don'kno(h)w.", said with laugh tokens, conveys both his appreciation of the humor and an equally mock doubt about the teacher's subject matter, displaying agreement with the radio host's stance that the teacher seems to be confusing history with divinity.

5.4 Alternative question error corrections in pedagogy

In pedagogical situations, it is quite common for teachers to use alternative questions to initiate error correction on both student's prior talk and on portions of student's' written text, and on both language and content. Parents can also use these questions in pedagogical activities with their children. These alternative questions are thus "known-information questions" (Mehan 1979b), questions to which the teacher/parent knows the answer. Pedagogically, the alternative questions function to elicit learner correction and to guide learners to the correct answer. Variations range from conversation-like repair initiations, as in Excerpt 63 above, to practices that are purely pedagogical.

5.4.1 Error correction initiated on student talk

The first example I discuss, from a one-on-one second language undergraduate writing conference, resembles conversational repair. This excerpt is taken from the same conference as Excerpts 41–44, discussed in Chapter 4. The student and teacher are discussing how to revise a draft of the student's paper on Charles de Gaulle's leadership. Zaleznik and Gardner are two authors from the class readings, to be used as sources for this essay. As this excerpt begins, the teacher, TC, is criticizing the organization of SD's text, saying that the section on "leadership through action rather than words," relates more closely to a discussion earlier in SD's essay than to the section on charismatic leadership, where it is located. The repair initiation occurs in lines 44–45 and 47.

```
(67)   TC/SD 8/11/96:34-36
       01  TC:    um: (0.5) up here you start talking
       02         about (1.0) followers, but then you
       03         just stop abruptly and then you
       04         talk about a whole nother
       05         explanation for leadership.
       06         (0.5)
       07         which is through action rather than
       08         words. .h [which is going back to
       09                   [((turns back to page 1))
       10         that (.) main point that I thought
       11         you were trying to make up here.
       12         (0.5)
       13  SD:    °(yeah?)°
       14         (1.5)
       15  TC:    an you just said you wanted
```

```
16              [to talk about the story (.) the
17  SD:         [((sniff))
18  TC:         direct leadership mainly and
19              charismatic leade[rship later.
20  SD:                          [°yeah°
21  TC:         but you're doing the opposite here.
22              (0.8)
23                              [((SD lifts page))
24  SD:         but wasn't it [(.) this is one of
25              the ways that charismatic leaders
26              [um: use to: subtract ((attract))
27              [((TC turns page))
28  SD:         his followers?
29              (1.0)
30              showing the leadership (0.8)
31              through action?=rather- better than
32              words?
33              (2.0)
34  TC:         m::. so you're still talking about
35              charismatic leadership?
36              (0.5)
37  SD:         I don kno(huh huh)
38  TC:         is that what Zaleznik say:s?
39              (3.5)
40  SD:         ((smile voice from * to *))
41              *No::t really,
42              (1.2)
43              that's (.) that's my assumption,*
44  TC: -->     .h wul- (0.2) I mean- (0.2) that's
45      -->     your assumption?=or [did you <get
46  SD:                             [yeah:
47  TC: -->     that> from one of the articles.=
48  SD:         =ahm not sure heh [heh ((sniff))
49  TC:                           [cause this is
50              really what Gardner's talking
51              abo[ut.
52  SD:            [yeah?
53              (1.0)
54  TC:         I mean (.) that actually this kind
55              of thing is an indirect leadership.
56              =right?
57              (6.5)
58              the person who embodies a story,
```

TC is criticizing the organization of SD's paper, based on the organization that SD, himself, has proffered (lines 1–21). In defending his organization, SD claims that "leadership through action rather than words" is one of the ways that charismatic leaders attract their followers (lines 24–32). TC then questions this interpretation of charismatic leadership with a yes/no RPQ, asking "is that what Zaleznik say:s?" (line 38). SD agrees that this idea was not from Zaleznik (line 41) and adds that it's his assumption (line 43), i.e., his own idea. This claim is also questioned by TC with an alternative question, prefaced by two abandoned beginnings: ".h wul- (0.2) I mean- (0.2) that's your assumption?=or did you <get that>from one of the articles." (lines 44–45, 47).

TC's disagreement with SD's claim is done in the form of other-initiated repair. The first alternative contains a repetition of the student's prior turn, containing the trouble source, with change of deictic reference and with upward intonation: "that's your assumption?" The second alternative provides the candidate correction, "or did you <get that>from one of the articles." "Assumption" and "articles", the two lexical items that contain the disputed information, are given contrastive stress. That TC intends the second alternative to be the correct one is shown in lines 49–51, where she gives an account for her claim embedded in the second alternative: "cause this is really what Gardner's talking about." She is claiming that SD's idea is from one of the other class readings by Gardner. TC's turn is also done in a dispreferred manner, delayed within her turn by "wul-", pauses, and "I mean-", further displaying its status as a disagreement with SD.

SD at first orients to TC's unfolding turn as a yes/no question providing a candidate hearing for confirmation. He answers the first alternative with "yeah:" (line 46), confirming the hearing. However, he later backs down from an agreement with this alternative on hearing the second alternative (line 48). SD's backdown demonstrates his orientation to the second alternative as a candidate correction. It would be difficult for SD to accept the correction as stated because it would suggest that he had given wrong information about his source in the prior turn. What he can do, however, is to display that he is now less certain where he got the idea.

5.4.2 Error correction initiated on student writing

Teachers can also use alternative questions to initiate error correction on student writing. This variation of the practice has many similarities to correction of student talk done as other-initiated repair, discussed in Excerpt 67, but it differs from repair as defined by conversation analysts in that it does not target a trouble source in prior talk but in the written text. When this type of error correction is used in certain kinds of pedagogical activities, it may differ from repair in yet another way. Often in writing conferences teachers and students devote portions of the conference to language error correction. When alternative question error corrections are used in these portions of the conference, as in the excerpt below, they do not interrupt the ongoing course of action to initiate repair, as does conversational repair, but they *are* the mainline course of action. In the following excerpt, the teacher has been reading the student's text aloud, eliciting error corrections as she reads. The student is gazing at the same text. The teacher has just finished one error correction segment and is moving on to the next error in the text:

```
(68)    TT/SA11/15/96:33
        01 TT:      okay,
        02          (3.0)
        03 TT: -->  whe:n or if:.
        04          (1.8)
        05 SA:      i:f.
        06          (0.2)
        07 TT:      mm hmm
        08          (0.8)
```

Despite the difference in medium and the ongoing task of error correction in which this turn occurs, the alternative question in this excerpt works in a very similar way to the question in Excerpt 67. The first alternative targets the trouble source, "when", in this case, by reading it from the student's written text. This reading functions like the conversational repair practice of targeting a trouble source in a prior turn by repeating it. The second alternative similarly provides the candidate correction: "if". Both SA (line 5) and TT (line 7) orient to this second alternative as the correct answer.

5.4.3 Evidence for canonical order of alternatives

We have seen that, when alternative questions are used to initiate error correction, the order of the two alternatives is significant. The first alternative targets a trouble source, either by repeating a portion of the student's prior talk or reading a portion of the student's text, calling it into question and conveying that it should be reconsidered; the second offers the candidate correction. We have also seen that participants orient to this ordering as canonical by treating the second alternative as the *preferred* one. Additional evidence that participants orient to this as the canonical order comes from the following excerpt, where the teacher produces an alternative question that reverses the order of the two alternatives (line 14). Although the teacher's turn is not used to elicit correction of a prior item, as do alternative question error corrections, the fact that it is done in a correction-relevant environment leads to some confusion. The excerpt is taken from an ESL reading class. The teacher is leading a student discussion about the characters in the novel they are reading.

(69)　MGLIT 7/18/00
```
01  TM:        he is cold. yeah.=ar or he's cool,
02             alright, (.) he's cool <he pretends
03             he likes her, (0.5) but what's his
04             emotional state. what's his
05             feeling.=he's indifferent, what
06             goes with that.
07             (0.2)
08  S6:        bor[ing,
09  TM:           [he's bored.
10  TM:        bo::[red,
11  S?:            [bored.
12  S?:        bo[red or.
13  S5:          [bo::red.
14  TM:   -->  is he bor[ed or boring.
15  S?:                 [(       )
16             ((chorus of students give answer))
17  S?:        [bored
18  S2?:       [bor[ing.
19  S5?:           [bored.
20  S?:        huh huh
21             (0.5)
22  TM:        he's bored.
23  S?:        bored. [( )
24  S?:               [bored.
25  TM:                [he's bored.
```

When one student offers "boring" as a description of one of the characters (line 8), in response to the teacher's elicitation, the teacher corrects it to "bored." (line 9), placing extra stress on the correction, as she hears the student's error. She then repeats the correction after the overlap, again with special prosodic marking, a lengthening of the vowel (line 10). After several student repetitions of "bored" (lines 11–13), the teacher asks an alternative question, "is he bored or boring." (line 14). This question is not done as a repair of an immediately prior utterance, as students are repeating the correction accurately. Rather, the teacher seems to be checking to see whether all students have understood the correct form. In formulating this question, the teacher puts the correct choice first and the wrong one last. Unfortunately, in this environment, where error correction is on the table, the teacher's turn is likely to be heard as an alternative question error correction initiation. Before the alternative question, students were all repeating the correct answer, "bored." After the alternative question, however, there was some confusion, with at least one student repeating the incorrect alternative, "boring", necessitating a repetition of the correct alternative (lines 22 and 25).

5.4.4 Providing candidate corrections after student failure to self-correct

The design of alternative questions used to target errors and present candidate corrections allows teachers to retroactively convert turns that merely target a trouble source into alternative question error corrections. Teachers can do this by adding the second alternative as an increment when students display problems self-correcting. These turns can therefore function in a similar way whether they are designed from the beginning as alternative questions or the second alternative is added after a recipient's silence. The next excerpt from a one-on-one writing conference provides an example of this latter practice. The excerpt begins with the teacher reading from the student's text. The teacher and student are sitting side-by-side, both with eyegaze on the text.

```
(70)   TT/SA11/15/96:6
       12 TT:     ((reading from SA's text))
       13         "a potential affec[tive"
       14 SA:                      [(°     °)
       15         (0.2)
       16 TT: ->  a:ffective?
       17         (0.2)
       18 TT: ->  or e[ffective.
       19 SA:        [(arc) effective.
       20 TT:     effective. mm hmm (.hh) leader.
       21         however his
```

The teacher interrupts her reading of the student's text with a short silence (line 15), which, by the way, can give the student a chance to provide a correction if he sees the error. Following this silence, she produces an utterance which targets an element of the prior spoken text as a trouble source by repeating it with upward intonation: "a:ffective?" (line 16). This utterance also resembles the first alternative in an alternative question error correction. The way she produces this repetition provides an additional hint about the nature of the problem; she stresses and lengthens the first syllable, which is the problematic syllable. The turn is followed by a short silence during which the student has another more explicit opportunity to self-correct, but does not (line 17). Although this silence is very brief, it can be understood as an indication that the student does not immediately realize what the problem is. The teacher then provides the student with the correct answer itself, in a turn designed as an increment to the prior utterance, a turn which resembles the second alternative of an alternative question (line 18). As she begins the correct alternative, again stressing the first syllable, the only syllable that differs from the trouble source, the student enters in overlap with the correction. In this case, the teacher's turn was not designed from the outset as an alternative question error correction, but was retroactively made into one after the student demonstrated problems providing an immediate correction. Adding the second alternative as an increment after student silence provides the student with the correct answer itself, though it is done as a *candidate* correction, leaving it up to him to choose it. Also, because it retroactively changes the student's silence after the first question into the teacher's intra-turn pause, it can disguise the student's inability to self-correct.

5.4.5 Disambiguating the first alternative

The second alternative not only provides the students with a candidate correction; it can also clarify the function of the first alternative, especially when there is potential for confusion with more common conversational repair initiations that present candidate hearings. When portions of student writing are targeted in the first alternative, as in Excerpts 68 and 70, the ongoing sequential environment of error correction and the fact that the targeted item is available to both parties convey that there is something problematic about that portion of text. The first alternative is thus unambiguously heard as targeting an error for correction, even before the second alternative is presented. However, when teachers target prior student *talk* for correction, the function of an utterance that merely targets a trouble source in the prior talk, without offering a candidate correction, is not always clear. Although teachers sometimes add contrastive stress and exaggerated intonation, which can convey that there is a problem with the targeted portion of talk, as in Excerpt 17, Chapter 2 ("daughters:"), these cues are not always present, and in spite of the teacher's epistemic authority, these repair initiations are not always heard as invitations to self-correct. Sometimes they are heard as candidate hearings proffered for confirmation, as we already saw in the discussion of SD's response to TC's pre-disagreement in Excerpt 16, Chapter 2, reprinted below:

(71) **TC/SD 8/11/96:7**
```
87 TC:      It's background?=
88 SD: -->  =yeah.=
```

SD simply confirms TC's repair as if it were a candidate hearing.

We also saw how, in Excerpt 67, SD similarly responds (in overlap) to the first alternative as if it were a candidate hearing proffered for confirmation, rather than the initiation of a correction sequence (line 46). It is only after he hears the second alternative that he backs down from his earlier position (line 48):

```
44 TC:      .h wul- (0.2) I mean- (0.2) that's
45          your assumption?=or [did you <get
46 SD: -->                      [yeah:
47 TC:      that> from one of the articles.=
48 SD: -->  =ahm not sure heh [heh ((sniff))
```

In this case the second alternative seems to have disambiguated the first alternative, making it clear that it functioned to target and question a trouble source in the student's prior talk rather than to provide a candidate understanding of the prior talk.

Both the potential for disambiguation with the second alternative, and the relationship between the practices of targeting a trouble source for self-correction and alternative question error corrections, are nicely illustrated in the following excerpt, taken from a parent/child interaction in the home.[46] The mother is a native speaker of Korean, and has lived in the U.S. for several years. She is bilingual in English and Korean. The daughter, around 3 years old at the time, is also growing up bilingual. Prior to this exchange, the daughter had been having problems confusing the words "glue" and "blue", and the mother and daughter had practiced pronouncing the more difficult word "glue". The following excerpt was recorded while the mother and daughter were playing together, cutting out pictures and gluing them on blank sheets of paper. The daughter had just cut out a picture of one of her favorite cartoon characters, "Blue," and was about to glue it onto the plain paper.

(72) **Kay and Daughter 2002**
```
01 Child:       I need some more blue:.
02 Mom:   -->   you need some more blue?
03 Child:       uh huh,
04 Mom:   -->   you need some more blue:?
```

```
05                  or glue:.
06  Child:          glue.
07  Mom:            glue?
08  Child:          yap.
```

In this context, it is clear that the daughter means "glue" rather than "blue". When the daughter first mispronounces the word "glue", the mother presents her with an opportunity to self-correct by repeating the turn with upward intonation and change of deictic pronoun (line 2). The daughter, however, seems to understand this repetition as a candidate hearing proffered for confirmation, rather than an opportunity to self-correct, and confirms the hearing (line 3). The mother then tries a second prompt using an alternative question. The first alternative (line 4) repeats her prior repair initiation, but with additional stress on the error, and the second alternative (line 5) provides a candidate correction, also with contrastive stress. Using an alternative question makes it possible for the mother to contrast the two forms that the daughter has a history of confusing, and this time the daughter understands the problem and is able to make the correction (line 6). When the mother subsequently repeats the daughter's response, most likely to reinforce the correct pronunciation, the daughter confirms the correct choice (line 8).

5.4.6 Variations on alternative question error corrections

Having seen the relationship of the first alternative to a repair that targets a trouble source for self-correction, we can now see how a variation on the alternative questions discussed above can be employed to do slightly different work. In the following two excerpts from the same writing conference, the teacher uses two different alternative questions to initiate error correction on a portion of student text. In both examples, as in Excerpt 70, the questions are not designed from the outset as alternative questions but become so retroactively when the teacher adds an increment to the first question in the form of an alternative choice. These questions differ from the alternative questions discussed above, however, in the design of the first alternative. Rather than repeating a portion of a prior utterance, the first alternative is designed as a yes/no RPQ of the type discussed in Chapter 4. It indirectly criticizes the text by pointing to a problem. The second alternative further specifies the problem.

The teacher, TT, and student, SR, are discussing a draft of SR's essay on Adolf Hitler's leadership. They are going through SR's text at SR's request, trying to determine if the quotes he uses at the end of each paragraph are appropriate summaries of the content of that paragraph. After SR negatively evaluates his first quote, TT convinces him that that quote *is* appropriate, but she then goes on to suggest a slight revision of the content of the paragraph to make his main point more explicit. She introduces this suggestion with a yes/no question to which she adds a series of increments, the final increment converting the yes/no question to an alternative question.

(73)   TT/SR11/15/96: 22-23
```
01 TT:  -->  'nkay. >have you made a big enough
02      -->  poi:nt he:re (.h) in this section
03      -->  where you've been talking about
04      -->  (.h) all the things he promised
05      -->  in his speeches.
06           (0.8)
07 TT:  -->  tha:t (0.5) that this really (0.5)
08      -->  excited people.
09           (0.5)
10 TT:  -->  that this (0.5) generated strong
11      -->  (.) emotions in people.
12           (1.0) ((after 0.8 seconds, and
13                 overlapping with TT's next turn, SR
14                 does lateral headshake))
15 TT:  -->  or is that implied.
16           (0.5)
17 SR:       implied.
18           (0.5)
19 TT:       okay.
20           (0.2)
21 TT:       so ma[y
22 SR:           [so I should (0.5) probably
23            (0.8) add u- explain some more.
24            (0.2)
25 TT:       mm hmm. (.hh) yeah this choice of
26           the word that everyone from young
27           and o:ld (0.5) could relate to.
28           (.h) that relate to is kind of
29           (0.2) that has no: (0.5) positive
30           (0.5) connotation.=it has no
31           positive meaning.=it's just a
32           neutral (0.8) it's kind of a
33           neutral word.=I can relate to that
34           means I can understand that.
```

After TT and SR discuss the main point of the paragraph in question and determine that the final quote is appropriate, TT closes that discussion with "°nkay." and goes on to ask a yes/no question about this paragraph: ">have you made a big enough poi:nt he:re (.h) in this section where you've been talking about (.h) all the things he promised in his speeches." (lines 1–5). The fact that the teacher returns to the discussion of the paragraph in question after approving the quote at the end could already suggest that there is something problematic about this paragraph. Otherwise, why ask the question at this point? Because of where it is placed sequentially, and perhaps also because of its sentence-final intonation, this question can convey a stance that the student did not, actually, "make a big enough point" here.

SR does not immediately respond to this question (line 6) as an RPQ, with the typical aligning "no" answer discussed in Chapter 4. Earlier, TT had insisted that SR try to determine himself whether or not the ending quotes were adequate summaries. She said that he should not be depending on her to make this assessment for him. SR may, therefore, be treating this as another "real" question, and taking time to evaluate the paragraph for himself. His eyegaze is on his text.

TT then continues by adding an increment to the original question in the form of a relative clause: "tha:t (.05) that this really (0.5) excited people." (lines 7–8). This increment helps to clarify what TT sees as missing. It is followed by a .5 second pause (line 9), during which SR again fails to respond. TT then adds another relative clause increment: "that this (0.5) generated strong (.) emotions in people." (lines 10–11), further clarifying what is missing. Again, there is at first no response. As SR begins to shake his head "no", TT adds the final increment, in the form of a second alternative, turning the turn retroactively into an alternative question: "or is that implied." (line 15). This addition further specifies the problem. SR has merely "implied" the point of the paragraph summarized in the final quote. He needs to make the point more explicit.

SR answers TT's question by choosing the obviously *preferred* alternative (line 17) and TT confirms this choice as correct (line 19). After SR formulates an understanding of how he should revise the paper, TT goes on to further specify that the problem is one of word choice.

In the following excerpt, TT and SR are engaged in the same activity. They have been working on the next paragraph of SR's text and have just decided that that paragraph discusses the common goal Hitler shared with his followers: rebuilding Germany. At the beginning of this excerpt, TT reads the quote that concludes the paragraph. She then implies, with an alternative question (lines 8–12), that the quote does not adequately summarize the paragraph.

(74)   TT/SR11/15/96:27-28
```
01 TT:      (.hh) ((reading)) "Hitler is indeed
02          a great leader because he not only
03          mobilized his followers toward a
04          common goal but also significantly
05          influenced their thoughts behaviors
06          and feelings of his followers.
07          (3.5) ((TT'sgaze remains on paper))
08 TT: -->  allright. have you said that.
09          (0.5)
10 TT: -->  y- (0.5) in this.=or have you been
11     -->  really just talking about the
12     -->  common (1.5) common goal.
13          (1.5)
14 SR:      °oh:. okay.°
15          (2.2)
16 ??:      °mm::°
17          (3.0)
18 SR:      n::. okay so I should probably
19          (0.5) like e- be- (.) before I
20          introduce this one, I should (0.8)
21          probably explain a li- little
22          bit more.
23 TT:      (.hh) >yeah< it seems to me that
24          [(0.2) like
25          [((TT lifts gaze from paper))
26          (0.2) if we look at some leaders
27          like (1.5) li:ke (.) Ho Chi Min,
28          you know, they were (0.5) were
29          talking about (0.2) >we read<
30          that paper [about (.hh) Ho.
```

The first alternative, "allright. have you said that." (line 8) is done as a freestanding yes/no question. It is similar to TJ's question in Excerpt 39: "didja tell me that?". As an RPQ, it targets SR's final quote for criticism, implying "you didn't say, in this paragraph, what you just said in your summary quote; the quote doesn't therefore adequately summarize the paragraph." In this example, it may again be unclear to SR that this is an RPQ because of TT's earlier insistence that SR try to determine himself whether or not the ending quotes are adequate summaries. From SR's perspective, this may be a question that encourages him to evaluate the end quote himself. Perhaps because of this ambiguity, the question is followed by a .5 second silence (line 9) during which SR does not respond. TT then continues by adding two increments to the first question, first, a prepositional phrase, and then a second alternative: "y- (0.5) in this.=or have you been really just talking about the common (1.5) common goal." (lines 10–12). The latter increment characterizes this turn, retroactively, as an alternative question. As such, it disambiguates the first alternative, showing that it was, indeed targeting a problem. The second alternative also contains two items, *really* and *just*, which help to convey the stance that it is the correct alternative.

SR eventually responds to the alternative question as if it were an assertion, rather than a question: "°oh:. okay.°" (line 14). The "oh" displays that he has learned new information (Heritage 1984a), and the "okay" accepts this information (Schegloff 1995b, to appear). SR and TT then go on to discuss how to revise the paragraph.

In the following excerpt, yet another type of alternative question is used. The first alternative (lines 3–6) targets a trouble source in the student's text. However, it does not directly question that portion of student text by repeating it, as in Excerpts 68 and 70. It targets the trouble source by providing a possible account for the student's grammar decision, and at the same time, questions this account. The second alternative (line 6) provides the correct answer, but not by providing an alternative choice. It provides the correct answer by negating the first alternative.

(75)   TT/SA11/15/96:29-30
```
02                  (2.8)
03 TT:   -->  >okay< an' then: (.) he:re, (1.0)
04       -->  >okay< is germany one of the
05       -->  countries that ha:s (0.5) a the:
06       -->  in front of it? or not.
07                  (1.5)
08 TT:        the united states because it's
09            plural.=
10 SA:        =mm hmm
11 TT:        the soviet union,=because you've got
12            (.) sovie[t
13 SA:                 [soviet.
14            (0.2)
15 SA:        so
16 TT:        but
17            (0.5)
18 SA:        u (hh)I (0.2) don't have to use
19            [the (    )
20 TT:        [no:. right. uh huh,
```

After several additional hints (lines 8–9, 11–12) and a contrastive conjunction (line 16), the student makes the correct answer explicit in lines 18–19, and his answer is confirmed as correct (line 20).

5.5 Recognizing the actions performed by alternative question repairs

We saw earlier how adding the second alternative can disambiguate a turn when the first alternative is in danger of being heard as a candidate understanding proffered for confirmation. Here I discuss in more detail how recipients recognize what action alternative question repairs are performing, i.e., whether they are presenting two candidate hearings/understandings or a candidate correction. This is not a problem with alternative questions used to initiate error correction on student writing. In this case, the first alternative targets what the student wrote and can obviously not be one of two alternate understandings. There is a potential problem, however, with repair initiations on prior talk. How does the recipient know whether or not these are meant to be "real," information-seeking questions, i.e., presenting two possible hearings for clarification, or RPQs that offer candidate corrections of a prior utterance?

Before we consider this question, however, we need to ask whether this is a dilemma that participants themselves actually orient to or merely an analyst's problem. Some evidence that it is important for participants is that the two types of actions can make relevant different responses. Alternative question repair initiations that present two alternate hearings or understandings make relevant a response that simply repeats one of the alternate hearings (see Excerpts 60 and 62), either alone or embedded in a repetition of the original utterance. In contrast, the relevant response to an alternative question error correction varies, depending on whether the recipient chooses the candidate correction or rejects it. As we saw in the discussion of Excerpt 63, a rejection of the candidate correction can take on characteristics of a dispreferred response, i.e., done with delays and accounts.

How then do recipients recognize the difference between alternative question repairs that present alternate hearings/understandings for clarification and those that present candidate corrections? An obvious answer would be that when two alternatives are presented that are hearably similar, the repair is heard as presenting two alternate hearings for clarification, as in Excerpts 59 and 60. When the two alternatives repeat terms that were both present and confused in the prior talk, the repair is heard as eliciting clarification about which term was intended, as in Excerpt 62. Finally, when the two alternatives are not hearably similar, and the person who initiates the repair has epistemic authority, i.e., can claim some prior knowledge about which of the alternatives is the correct one, the repair is heard as a candidate correction.

Although this solution seems obvious, the reality is actually somewhat more complex. The two alternatives in Excerpt 72, "blue" and "glue" are hearably similar, yet they elicit self-correction rather than a repetition of the item actually said. It can also be argued that, to a non-native speaker of English, "he" and "she" are phonologically similar, yet in Excerpt 62, SJ produces a correction rather than repeating the pronoun he actually said in the immediately preceding talk, even though TJ does not seem to be proffering a candidate correction. In Excerpt 72, the fact that the alternative question is the second repair initiation on the same item, along with the daughter's history of confusing the two terms, evidently enables the daughter to rethink her prior utterance and discover the error. In Excerpt 62, when TJ contrasts the two pronouns, it seems to bring the confusion to SJ's attention, a circumstance that he expresses with the change-of-state token "oh"(Heritage 1984a), and enables him to self-correct. Participants may orient to alternative question repairs as alternative hearings when possible, i.e., when they present two hearably similar alternatives and when there is, in fact, no known error. However, when alternative question repair initiations make recipients aware of errors in their prior utterance by contrasting two forms that have been confused, as in Excerpts 62 and 72, even when they are hearably similar, this provides an opportunity for recipients to correct their errors.

When it is not possible to hear the two alternatives as alternate possible hearings or understandings of the prior talk, i.e., when they are not either hearably similar, or both evoked in the prior talk, it is possible to hear these repairs as candidate corrections, whether or not they were intended as such, even if no error has in fact been made and the person initiating repair does not have the requisite knowledge to claim that an error has been made. In Excerpt 63, even though Libby is discussing articles that only she has read and Tamar did not have access to, and there is nothing in the prior talk to lead Tamar to think that Libby did, in fact, mean "abridged" rather than "revised", Libby still demonstrates that she hears Tamar's turn as a correction. In this case, the turn design is more powerful than Tamar's (lack of) epistemic authority in projecting a possible action.

5.6 Summary and discussion

In this chapter I have discussed an other-initiated repair practice, using the form of an alternative question, and the various actions that this practice accomplishes. Alternative question repair initiations can present alternate hearings or understandings of a prior utterance for clarification. In this case there is no structural preference for one of the two alternatives over the other. Alternative questions can also be used to initiate error correction by targeting a trouble source with the first alternative and providing a candidate correction with the second. In this case, they are RPQs that convey the epistemic stance of the questioner: the second alternative is the "preferred" one. Rejection of the "preferred" alternative can therefore be done in a way that reflects its status as a dispreferred response.

Pedagogically, the alternative questions function to elicit student correction and guide students to the correct answer. The second alternative provides the student with the correct answer, though in the form of a *candidate* correction. It is up to the student to choose the second alternative as the correct one.

When teachers or parents use alternative questions to initiate error correction on learners' talk, the practice can resemble conversational repair, although the action it performs is not common in mundane conversation. When teachers use alternative questions to initiate error correction on student writing, this practice differs from conversational repair in two ways. First, it does not target a trouble source in prior talk but in the written text. And second, when alternative question error corrections are performed in segments of talk devoted to correcting errors in the student's written text, the alternative question sequences do not interrupt the ongoing course of action to initiate repair, as does conversational repair. They *are* the mainline course of action. These portions of the conference are made up of sequences devoted solely to error correction, and when these sequences are initiated by alternative questions, the entire sequence, or course of action, is devoted to the repair.

The design of alternative questions used to target a trouble source and provide candidate corrections allows teachers to convert turns which merely target a trouble source into alternative question error corrections by adding the second alternative as an increment when students display problems self-correcting. These turns can therefore function in a similar way whether they are designed from the beginning as alternative questions or the second alternative is added after a recipient's silence. Also, because it retroactively changes the student's silence after the first question into the teacher's intra-turn pause, it disguises the student's inability to self-correct.

When error correction is initiated on talk, as opposed to written work, adding a second alternative can clarify that a candidate correction, rather than a candidate hearing, is being proffered, especially in a pedagogical environment of ongoing error correction. Providing a second alternative, especially if it cannot be understood as an alternate hearing, is to propose that the first alternative be reconsidered in favor of the second. Even when the two alternatives are hearable similar, recipients can still hear the second as a candidate correction if the practice contrasts two forms that they are aware of confusing. When the two alternatives are not hearably similar, recipients are more likely to understand the second alternative as a candidate correction.

The pedagogical use of alternative questions to elicit student corrections and guide students to correct answers might be considered an extension of the conversational preference for self-correction (Schegloff et al. 1977). However, given the asymmetry of knowledge (Drew & Heritage 1992a) between teachers and learners, teachers could choose to display their epistemic authority by correcting learners' errors explicitly. Yet they often choose a type of pedagogy that allows the learners to display their own understanding of the corrections they need to make. This choice of error correction practices, and its relationship to the culture of teaching in North America, will be discussed in more detail in Chapter 6.

CHAPTER 6

Conclusion

6.1 Summary of findings

We have seen how conversationalists can use questions to convey assertions that perform a variety of related actions: challenges to a recipient's actions in the exogenous context; challenges to a prior turn, either that of a co-present party or the reported speech of a non-present party; pre-disagreements; prompts for self-correction of errors; and, in pedagogical situations, criticisms of student text and hints to enable learners to perform error correction. The use of these practices to do challenging in ordinary conversation is possibly universal, as evidenced by examples from Korean and Kalili speech communities. As we will see, however, their use in pedagogical situations to elicit error correction does not seem to be universal.

Many of the questions discussed in this book are known as *rhetorical questions*. I have used the term *reversed polarity questions*, or *RPQs*, to refer to these questions for two main reasons. First, the term *rhetorical questions* can be somewhat misleading. It suggests that these questions do not receive answers. As we have seen, many of these questions do, in fact, receive answers. What they have in common is that they are heard as asserting opinions rather than as seeking new information. When answers are given, they are designed to either align or disalign with the assertion conveyed through the *RPQ*. The term *RPQ* also captures the relationship among a wider variety of questions, those that are commonly thought of as *rhetorical* and similar *reversed polarity questions* used as pre-disagreements or to elicit error correction.

When RPQs are used to challenge prior turns, they refer anaphorically back to the claim they are challenging, using substitution, incorporating elements of the prior claim into their design, or using adjacent positioning in the next turn. At times speakers latch on to their questions, without the small beat of silence that normally comes after a grammatically-complete utterance, an increment-like addition, a "because" clause (cf. Ford 1993). This "because" clause provides an account for the assertion conveyed in the RPQ, for example, from TC in Excerpt 28: "ok how's it background.=because I- like .h most people wouldn't know maybe what he meant by direct indirect ordinary innovative or visionary." This increment-like addition does not fit grammatically and semantically with the question, but with the assertion that it conveys, i.e., "it's not background because most people wouldn't know what he meant. . . ."

Responses to RPQs orient to the actions they are being used to perform. Different actions and different sequential contexts make different responses relevant. Challenges can be responded to with disagreements, especially in news interviews, or with backdowns. Students most often respond to criticisms of their text with answers that agree with the criticism, and disagreements are done as dispreferred responses. In contrast, the preferred response to a hint is the correct answer that it was used to elicit. The preferred response for alternative questions used to elicit error correction is to choose the second alternative, the candidate correction.

RPQ challenges used in institutional settings orient to institutional roles and norms and can help accomplish institutional goals, even when their design and the actions they accomplish are similar, both in and outside of the specific institutional settings. Much of the conversation analytic work on talk in institutional settings focuses on institutionally specific practices which help define talk in particular settings (cf. Drew & Heritage 1992a). As important as this work is, the analysis of RPQ challenges in institutional settings reminds us that institutional norms and roles can be oriented to and institutional goals accomplished by means of practices of talk which are not, themselves, institutionally specific, and which may accomplish similar work across a broad range of settings. The work done by these types of practices in one setting can be informed by investigating the practice in a broad range of contexts, including mundane conversation.

However, in Chapters 4 and 5 we also saw how the RPQ turns themselves, and the sequences of action in which the RPQs are used, can be designed to accomplish pedagogically specific goals, and how special inferential frameworks (Drew & Heritage 1992a; Levinson 1979) may be used in interpreting the actions that these RPQs accomplish. These RPQs can therefore be considered practices of pedagogical talk, rather than ordinary conversational practices which happen to be used in a pedagogical setting. For example, yes/no RPQs can be used in writing conferences to criticize student text or talk, pointing out what is problematic and suggesting a solution. We have seen how teachers' use of these RPQs in two different sequential contexts in this setting engenders different preferences for a response. We have also seen how alternative questions are used for pedagogical purposes to initiate error correction on learner talk and text, targeting the trouble source and providing a candidate correction.

Initiating error correction *in this manner*, with an alternative question RPQ, is not a common practice of mundane talk; rather, it is found almost exclusively in pedagogy and can help characterize this form of talk.

Although RPQs can contain lexical items such as *really* or negative polarity items such as *one jot* that could contribute to a polarity reversal, and some yes/no RPQs, especially prompts for self-correction, use contrastive stress or exaggerated intonation, many of these questions do not contain anything that could differentiate them in form or in intonation from regular information-seeking questions. With the exception of alternative question error corrections that provide two alternatives that are not hearably similar, it is not generally the design of an RPQ that contributes to a recipient's understanding of a particular question as an RPQ; it is the knowledge state of the questioner and the sequence of action in which the question is located. All three types of RPQs, yes/no, wh- and alternative question RPQs, are asked from positions of epistemic strength. Either the speakers have institutionally-oriented to claims to knowledge about the questions they are asking, as do broadcast news interviewers or teachers, or the question is asking about something already displayed to be in the speaker's knowledge domain.

Aside from epistemic strength, the sequential position of the questions also contributes to their being heard as RPQs. RPQs are more likely to be heard as challenges, rather than as information-seeking questions, when challenges would be expected responses, e.g., after accusations. For example, after Debbie's accusation that Shelley is "blowing off her girlfriends for guys", the question "when have I." is likely to be heard as a counter-challenge, i.e., "I never have." In pedagogical situations, after a student provides an answer to a *test* (Searle 1969) or *known information* (Mehan 1979b) question, one to which the teacher already knows the answer, there is an expectation that the teacher will evaluate that answer in the third turn (Mehan 1979b). Thus if a teacher initiates repair on a student's answer by repeating it with upward intonation, the teacher's epistemic authority, together with the fact that this repair appears in the *evaluation* position, will often convey to students that their answer was problematic. If an RPQ is asked after an answer is elicited from a student and the student displays trouble answering correctly, e.g., "just saved?", RPQs in this sequential position can be heard as hints to enable the student to achieve a correct answer. In writing conferences, yes/no RPQs are likely to be heard as criticisms of student text after a portion of text has been problematized. For the teacher to ask "is it clear?" conveying the possibility that the portion of text he had just characterized as problematic was, in fact, clear, would make no sense in this sequential context. Only a negative assertion, "It's not clear," would further the course of action established at the beginning of the sequence. Finally, when alternative questions are used in error correction sequences, the first alternative is not likely to be confused with a candidate understanding proffered for confirmation.

6.2 Using questions rather than statements

If reversed polarity questions accomplish the actions they do because they convey assertions of the opposite polarity to that of the question, why use questions rather than simply the corresponding assertion? What difference does the question form make? The answer to this question varies, depending on the setting and the action being performed with the question. It is easier to answer for RPQs used by professionals, i.e., news interviewers or teachers, in institutional settings.

6.2.1 Challenges by broadcast news interviewers

We have already seen that the question form solves a problem for broadcast news interviewers. As discussed earlier, broadcast news interviewers operate under two competing norms (Heritage 2002a). On the one hand, they are expected to take an impartial, objective, "neutralistic" stance toward interviewees (Clayman 1988; Heritage & Greatbatch 1991), not offering their own opinions; on the other hand, they ascribe to a "norm of adversarialness" which challenges their interviewees. RPQs are the ideal form for meeting expectations of both norms. Because of their ability to convey assertions, RPQs can be used to challenge interviewees. But because they are syntactic questions, interviewers can use them to maintain a fiction of neutrality, as in the following excerpt, discussed in (Heritage 2002a). The interviewer, Sam Donaldson, is interviewing Richard Darman, at the time a treasury official in the Bush, Sr. administration.

```
(76)  [US ABC This Week: October 1989: Darman]
      01 IR: --> Isn't it a fact, Mr. Darman,
      02          that the taxpayers will pay more
      03          in interest than if they just paid
      04          it out of general revenues?
      05 IE:     No, not necessarily. That's a
      06          technical argument--
      07 IR:     It's not a-- may I, sir?
      08          It's not a technical argument.
      09      --> Isn't it a fact?
```

```
10 IE:      No, it's definitely not a fact.
11          Because first of all,
12          twenty billion of the fifty
13          billion is being handled in
14          just the way you want - through
15          treasury financing.
16          The remaining--
17 IR: -->  I'm just asking you a question.
18     -->  I'm not expressing my personal
19     -->  views.
20 IE:      I understand.
```

After Donaldson asks an RPQ during two successive turns (lines 1 and 9), the interviewee exposes the assertion behind the question: "twenty billion of the fifty billion is being handled *in just the way you want* ..." (lines 12–14). Donaldson defends himself by asserting that he was "just asking ... a question" and "not expressing [his] personal views."

6.2.2 RPQ challenges in conversation

When RPQs are used to challenge others in mundane conversation, the reasons for their use are not as clear. Participants do use assertions to challenge prior claims. They deny the truth of the claim, as did Shelley in Excerpt 20 (line 33), reprinted below as Excerpt 77, or deny the claim itself, sometimes in addition to using an RPQ challenge (line 38):

(77) **Debbie and Shelley**
```
29 Deb:        =but if- but th- see this is
30             what I'm see:in. I'm seein well:
31             thats okay, but if Mark went you
32             would spend the mo::ney.
33 Shel: -->   ↑°no:, thats not true↑ either.=
34             ((begins soft, then rising))
35 Deb:        =I do'know,=jus don't blow off
36             your girlfriends for guy:s,
37             Shel.
38 Shel: -->   De:b I'm not. h[ow man-]e-
39 Deb:                        [o ka:y ]
40 Shel:      when have I.=beside ya- I mean
```

Why then use an RPQ challenge instead of, or in addition to, an assertion that denies the prior claim? One reason why wh-questions may be used is that they do more than simply deny the prior claim. They challenge the grounds for a prior claim, or action, implying that there are no adequate grounds for it, and therefore no basis for asserting the claim or doing the action in the first place. Wh-question challenges may also be more difficult to refute since a refutation would involve providing the grounds that the questioner implies are unavailable.

In a similar way, yes/no RPQ challenges in conversation may accomplish more than their corresponding assertion. Rather than simply expressing an opinion, they seem to be making a truth claim, and implying that that truth is known to the recipient. This claim can take on greater force than simply a denial. The questions are thus harder to refute. This may be why, according to Schieffelin (1990), they are used for disciplining children in Kaluli society. The shaming quality that these question have toward a child who has taken someone else's property and is asked "Is it yours to take?!" (85) may come from the fact that these questions refer to violated norms and the answer should be obvious to all present, including the sanctioned child. The questions are unanswerable, except as an admission of guilt.

6.2.3 Repetitions of a prior utterance, used as pre-disagreements and error correction initiations in mundane conversation

We have seen that RPQs, formatted as partial or full repeats of a prior utterance, can be used for doing pre-disagreements or error correction initiations. Although they are not done as syntactic questions but as "declarative questions" (Quirk et al. 1985; Weber 1993), it is useful to ask why they are done in this manner rather than as the corresponding assertion. Using an RPQ that does a partial repeat of another's previous utterance as the first element in a pre-disagreement sequence has the following advantage. Because the RPQ allows the questioner to convey an assertion "off the record," and avoid responsibility for making that assertion, it allows the possibility of a disagreement to be suggested, and, if that possibility is registered by the recipient, it allows the recipient to do a backdown, removing the need to do the actual disagreement, which would be a dispreferred action. Similarly, when repeats of a prior utterance are used to initiate error correction, they allow for the recipients to correct their own errors in the next turn, an action that is "preferred" over other-correction (Schegloff et al. 1977).

6.2.4 Pedagogical interactions

We have investigated several pedagogical practices that use RPQs to deal with learner errors. Each of these practices can also be done with a statement, rather than a question. In writing conferences yes/no RPQs are used by teachers to recall a violated norm, one that the students are expected to know. Through these RPQs, teachers diagnose problems and suggest solutions by associating a problematic portion of student text with an academic discourse norm. For example, the RPQ: "Didja tell me that?" conveys "You didn't say, in your text, what you just told me orally, but you should have." We have seen that the corresponding statement can also be used in performance evaluations. Jacoby and Gonzales (2002) show how the head of a physics research team uses negative observations such as "you didn't say that" to critique practice conference presentations by members of his team. These negative observations similarly convey that what the presenter said in clarification during the comment session should have been said earlier in the talk itself. However, they convey this information explicitly in statement form.

Error correction on prior talk or text can also be initiated inexplicitly by RPQs, or done explicitly. Teachers and parents use RPQs to initiate error correction on learner talk or writing by repeating a prior utterance or reading a portion of text, with upward intonation. This practice targets a trouble source for the student to correct. Alternative question error corrections are an extension of this practice. The first alternative similarly targets a trouble source; the second provides a candidate correction.

Although, as mentioned above, there is a conversational preference for self-correction (Schegloff et al. 1977), participants in conversation do at times explicitly correct another person's utterance, especially if the person doing the correction has epistemic authority, i.e., has a greater claim to knowledge. Here is an example of a conversational practice, discussed in Schegloff (1997a), that is similar to an alternative question repair initiation, although it is not, itself, an example of conversational repair.[47] It targets a trouble source and then provides a correction. But rather than providing a *candidate* correction, it does explicit error correction. A family has just sat down to dinner and plates are being passed for one of the party, Prudence, to dish out the main course.

```
(78)   Virginia
       01 MOM:      ˆJus' a ta::d. I been nibblin' while
       02           I was cookin' supper.
       03 PRU:      °uh hhuh ((laughter))
       04           (0.2)
```

```
05 MOM:        ˙hhh But Vuhginia is very hungry.
06             (1.9)
07 MOM:        Very very.
08             (1.9)
09 WES:        I thoughtju was diettin'.
10             (.)
11 VIR: -->    Me? No. Beth
```

In this example (line 11), Virginia first repeats the pronoun from Wesley's prior utterance with a change of deixis and with upward intonation, targeting that person reference as a trouble source. She follows this repetition with a rejection of the person reference, "No.", and a correction, substituting another person reference, "Beth". The turn thus begins with a repetition of an element in the prior talk, targeting it for correction, and continues with a rejection and replacement of that element, done as an explicit correction.

If performance critiques and error corrections are done explicitly as statements when the speaker has the epistemic authority, why, then, do teachers with epistemic authority often choose to do criticism and error correction indirectly, with yes/no RPQs, declarative questions that target the trouble source, and alternative questions that provide candidate corrections? I will suggest two reasons, both related to the professional culture of teaching in North America.

"Doing being teachers"
The use of RPQs in pedagogical interactions may relate to the perceived task and role of teacher in North American culture. That these teachers choose to do problem diagnosis and error correction in the form of questions may be one way for them to "do being teachers" within this cultural framework.

There seems to be a preference in middle-class North American culture, at least in some types of teaching sessions, for teaching by eliciting from the student rather than informing the student directly. This is related to a socialized pattern for learning through performance rather than observation, a pattern which Scollon and Scollon (1981) suggest is preferred in middle-class North American culture where the dominant, or expert, role is linked to spectatorship and the subordinate, or novice, role to exhibitionism. This pattern, to and through which members of the culture are socialized (Ochs & Schieffelin 1984), informs teacher-student roles, especially in second language instruction (Crago 1992; Poole 1992). Students are often expected to learn by displaying their abilities to the teacher rather than by observing teachers display their abilities. Teachers are expected to elicit student performance, and to assist students by means of scaffolding (Bruner 1975; Cazden 1988) to perform elicited tasks that are beyond their level of competence.[48]

This philosophy of teaching and learning clearly informs the overall organization of the writing classes in this study, with their emphasis on multiple drafts, done by the not-yet-competent novice, which the teacher/expert then assists the novice to revise in a one-on-one conference. This orientation toward learning is also evident in the talk itself. Much of the teacher talk is directed to eliciting answers from the students and assisting students to achieve those answers rather than giving students explicit information. This elicitation and assistance of student performance is often done by *known-information* questions which have been described as uniquely characteristic of teaching talk, both in and outside the classroom (Drew 1981; Mehan 1979b, 1985; Sinclair & Coulthard 1975).

RPQs, as we have seen, are a type of known-information question. Teachers demonstrate an orientation to RPQs as known-information questions by agreeing with or evaluating student answers as correct, an action commonly implemented in the third turn after correct answers to known-information questions (Mehan 1979a, 1985). Yes/no RPQs are used by teachers to assist student performance by pointing out what is problematic about a portion of student text and implying a remedy, while at the same time seeming to elicit this information from the student by means of a strongly preferred aligning response. Teachers also use yes/no RPQs as hints to elicit an answer when a student is unable to come up with a correct answer, instead of telling the student the answer. The design of an alternative question allows teachers to convey a correction, while at the same time presenting it as an option for the student to choose.

There is evidence that the use of known-information questions to elicit student performance is not characteristic of pedagogical interactions in all cultures, even some sub-cultures within North America, where the preferred manner of learning is through observation rather than performance (see, for example, Crago 1992; Heath 1983; Scollon & Scollon 1981). Using RPQs for diagnosing problems in performance and assisting students to achieve correct answers may be unique to pedagogical talk with clearly-defined teacher-student roles, at least within a North American cultural framework.

Mitigating criticism
Using questions to criticize student performance, rather than criticizing that performance directly, may also be seen by the teachers as a way of mitigating criticism. Earlier we looked at preference structure in terms of alternate pref-

erences for the second pair part. There are, however, not only preferred and dispreferred second pair parts; there are also preferred and dispreferred first pair parts; for example, offers are preferred over requests and noticing by others is preferred over announcements by self (Schegloff 1995b, to appear). Dispreferred first pair parts often show characteristics similar to those of dispreferred second pair parts. When other-corrections are done, for example, they are often modulated in form. One way in which this is done is by downgrading them epistemically by doing them as questions (Schegloff et al. 1977).

The fact that criticisms of student performance are done in question form as RPQs rather than done directly may, therefore, be in part because these actions are seen by teachers as dispreferred in spite of their centrality to pedagogy, and possibly to performance evaluations in general (Jacoby 1998). Explicit negative assessments in the physics lab comment sessions discussed by Jacoby (1998:406) were rare and confined almost solely to the principal investigator, Ron. And although Ron's comments were in general more direct than those of the other participants, even he avoided explicit negative assessments. For example, Ron's negative observations discussed earlier, e.g. "you didn't say that.", although they are heard as criticisms, are only criticisms by implication, implying "you should have said that."

Even though there may be some mitigation involved in doing criticism as a negative observation, the teachers in my study might still consider this form of criticism inappropriately direct. When Jacoby showed excerpts of the physics lab interactions to English as a second language teachers and teacher trainers, they were taken-aback by what they considered the directness of the criticisms, including those in the form of negative observations. Jacoby suggests that "long-standing ideologies in those professional cultures frown upon focusing on the negative aspects of a learner's or teacher-trainee's performance" (1998:314). In fact, as Jacoby says, some researchers working in this tradition have urged teachers and supervisors to avoid evaluative statements altogether (e.g. Fanselow 1988).

Paradoxically, however, in attempting to mitigate a dispreferred action by doing it in question form, teachers may inadvertently be performing another dispreferred action. There is a sense in which yes/no RPQs may convey a slight shaming quality (cf. Schieffelin's 1990 description of "confrontational rhetorical questions" used to discipline and shame young children in Kaluli society). If the criticism is done as an assertion, it is done as an informing, i.e., "You didn't tell me that." When done as an RPQ, however, i.e., "Did you tell me that?", the implication is that the students already know the answer to the question. A further implication may be that if the students already know what they have done wrong, they should not have made the mistake in the first place.

Problems with inexplicit nature of yes/no pedagogical RPQs
The use of RPQs to diagnose problems in a student's text has another drawback that is not found with the other pedagogical RPQs used to initiate error correction. This problem originates in the inexplicit nature of RPQs and in the preferred student response. We have already seen that it is possible for students to confuse repetitions of a prior utterance, intended to elicit error correction, with candidate understandings proffered for confirmation. However, teachers are made aware of this confusion when students simply confirm the hearing as correct, rather than correcting the targeted error.

Alternative questions used to elicit error correction are not likely to be misunderstood, especially when they provide two alternatives that cannot be heard as alternate hearings. Because alternative questions make relevant one of the two alternate hearings as a response, and the second alternative is clearly the candidate correction, error correction is accomplished when students respond with the correct alternative, although more discussion is often needed to show *why* that is the correct alternative.

Similarly, when yes/no RPQs are used as hints after students display problems answering a teacher's question, it is also easy for teachers to evaluate whether the practice has been effective. These questions make relevant the correct answer that the student originally had problems producing.

However, when yes/no RPQs are used to diagnose organizational problems in a student's text, it is difficult for teachers to evaluate, at that time, how effective the practice is in accomplishing their pedagogical goals. It is very easy for students to claim understanding with aligning "no" answers, and for teachers to assume that students understand, even when they do not. We saw in the analysis of Excerpt 38 how it is possible for a student to misunderstand the teacher's intent in using an RPQ. As was evident from his subsequent draft, the student heard "is that what this paper's about?" to be conveying "you need to provide the topic of the paper here" rather than "you need to provide a thesis statement here." The student's aligning answers to the two similar RPQs did not allow the teacher to detect this misunderstanding. It could only have been detected with a follow-up question, e.g., "Ok, how are you going to correct this sentence?", which the teacher did not provide.

A slightly different problem occurs in Excerpt 39. In the analysis of this RPQ sequence, I suggested that the teacher's use of a second RPQ is somewhat manipulative. The teacher responds to a student's dispreferred answer by reanalyzing the problem in a second RPQ, designed to get a preferred answer. This second RPQ gets an almost automatic "no" response:

```
152 TJ:   --> is it clear?
153 ST:       no
```

In fact, the response is almost too automatic. The preference structure, in this case, seems to have exerted such a strong force that the student complies rather automatically after attempting to disagree with the first RPQ. As we saw, in this case, it was the student, not the teacher, who was right. The teacher had misdiagnosed the problem.

This kind of automatic "no" response is commented on and criticized by a different teacher in the following excerpt. The RPQ in lines 2–4 gets an aligning response (line 5) even before the teacher is finished asking the question:

```
(79)  TT/SJ
      01  TT:      so you have to ma:ke (0.5) the
      02               logic here clear, is that clear do
      03               you think there?=with the-
      04               [i- the bridge?
      05  SJ:      [probably (not)
      06           (0.2)
      07  TT: --> well w- .h don't say probably
      08      --> not.=read it. hahaha[hahhhh .hh
      09  SJ:                         [hmhhhhhhh
      10                   [hh
      11  TT: --> [I don't want
      12      --> you to automatically say not.
```

These RPQs target complex organizational problems inexplicitly, and because they have such a clear preference for an aligning "no" answer that provides no information about how the RPQ was understood, second language students can easily recognize what is interactionally expected and can comply without understanding the implications of the RPQ. When students do not fully understand the norms that the RPQs target, their aligning answers can disguise this lack of understanding.

6.3 Final note

We saw in the discussion of repair initiations that recipients can make use of the turn design and context to figure out what action a repair initiation is being used to accomplish. As analysts we can often see their understanding of a particular repair initiation by how they respond to it. But this understanding can be at times equivocal, as we have seen in the discussion of Excerpts 56, 67, 69, and 71–75. This is because the same practice in the same sequential context can be used to do different actions. Schegloff (1997a: 520) discusses two kinds of equivocality in doing a CA analysis. One has to do with the analyst's skill or lack of access to the background to an interaction; the other with equivocality which is "internal to the data" , i.e., it is equivocality which is also present for the participants, themselves. As Schegloff reminds us, it is important that this latter equivocality not be rendered unequivocal in an analysis.

Appendix

Transcription symbols[49]

[ ]	Overlapping utterances
=	Latching: when there is no interval between adjacent utterances
(0.2)	Timed silence within or between utterances in tenths of a second
-	An abrupt cutoff of a word or sound
:	Extension of the sound
.	Falling intonation, e.g., final intonation.
,	Continuing intonation
?	Rising intonation
–	Stressed syllable
°	Quieter than surrounding talk
CAP	Louder than surrounding talk
↑↓	Marked change in pitch: upward or downward.
(h)	Aspirations
(.h)/.h	Inhalations
< >	Utterance is delivered at slower pace than surrounding talk
> <	Utterance is delivered at quicker pace than surrounding talk.
( )	Unclear hearing
(( ))	Comments, details of the scene
-->	Arrows in left-hand margin indicate focus of analysis

Notes

1. Conversation analytic (CA) transcription conventions, adapted from Atkinson and Heritage (1984:ix–xvi) are summarized in the Appendix. When portions of transcript are quoted in the text, punctuation within the quotation marks represents CA transcript conventions used in the transcripts.

2. For a more complete discussion, see Atkinson and Heritage (1984), Clayman and Gill (2004), Drew and Heritage (1992b), Heritage (1984b:Ch. 8), Levinson (1983:Ch. 6), and Zimmerman (1988).

3. See Schegloff (1995a) for a discussion of the relevance of "action" in CA research.

4. The pedagogically-specific practices I discuss are not restricted to institutional settings but can also be used to "do pedagogy" in the home, e.g., when parents initiate teaching interactions with their children. It is not the setting that constitutes the talk as pedagogical, but the type of activity that the participants are engaged in.

5. There are classes of motivated exceptions. For example, alignment with self-denigration or with compliments to oneself is a *dispreferred* response (Pomerantz 1984).

6. I thank John Heritage for access to the audiotape from this interview.

7. Other stance displays may also be expressed through these questions, but I am here concerned with how these questions display the epistemic stance of the speaker.

8. See Drew (1997) for a discussion of ways in which "open class" repair initiators such as "huh" may prefigure disaffiliation or disalignment between speakers.

9. John Heritage, in a personal communication, suggests that the assertions conveyed by these grammatically negative questions are treated by interviewers as matters of public record.

10. I am indebted to John Heritage for pointing out the connection between this demonstration of shifting epistemic environment and Bolinger's "blinds down" situation.

11. * Indicates throaty voice in this transcript. I thank Jenny Mandelbaum for the audiotape on which this transcript is based.

12. Since we do not have the beginning of this interaction, it is unclear what Joseph means in lines 16–19. I am treating this utterance as either a separate turn constructional unit or a grammatical increment to his claim in line 12. However, lines 16–19 could also be the beginning of the turn constructional unit in line 22, interrupted by Marcia in line 20. In this case, his question begins in line 16.

13. I thank Elinor Ochs for permission to use this data excerpt.

14. I thank Steve Clayman for this example.

15. For my own transcripts of pedagogical interactions, participants are labeled with two initials. The first, S or T, indicates whether they are a student or teacher. The second stands for their pseudonym.

16. When the teacher, as expert, suggests that a portion of SD's text is problematic, the preferred, or aligning, response would be a remedy, not a justification.

17. This question of audience is one that is routinely dealt with in college composition classes. Students who, as adult speakers, orient automatically to *recipient design* in their talk (Schegloff 1972), often need to be explicitly taught to design writing for a particular audience.

18. SD aligns by giving a clear and unmitigated "no" (cf. Koshik 2002a) but the (0.8) second delay suggests that he may be orienting to the dispreferred nature of the remainder of his turn.

19. Repairs are regularly initiated, however, when there is no external evidence of trouble in hearing or understanding previous talk.

20. It is also possible that a "how many …" question is more easily answered than the corresponding "when" question, even if it is with a guess. Shelley may therefore be self-correcting to a question that is less easily answered.

21. The interpretation of this question as a negative assertion may be strengthened by the negative polarity item *ever*. As discussed earlier, negative polarity items, also called "nonassertive forms" (Quirk et al. 1985), are words such as *any, anybody, ever, yet*, and phrases such as *at all, care to, say a word*, which are normally restricted to negative statements, i.e., statements which include words which are negative in form, such as *not, never, no, neither, nor*; or words which contain implied negatives, e.g. *just, before, fail, prevent, difficult*. When used in questions, they may therefore suggest a negative epistemic stance even when the questions do not contain grammatical negatives.

22. My thanks to Gene Lerner for permission to use this data segment.

23. Yoon (in progress) describes a number of similar yes/no and wh-RPQs used as complaints in Korean. In Yoon's Korean transcripts, the original utterances are followed by word-by-word interlinear glosses and, in bold and italics, the English translations. Dashes represent cut-off words or sounds, and hyphens represent morpheme boundaries.

24. In this respect, these questions differ from those discussed by Schegloff (1995b:75, to appear) that "can function doubly, both as actions in their own right and as vehicles or formats for other actions." Some questions, for example, may, in addition to requesting information, do other actions such as offers, as in "Would you like a cup of coffee?" Answers to these types of first pair parts, e.g., "yes, thank you," regularly address both the format, i.e., the question first, and then the action which is implemented through the question. However, the wh-questions I am concerned with here are not both requesting information and also doing challenging. Although they are grammatically formatted as questions, they seem to be doing challenging by conveying negative assertions, implying that the questions are unanswerable. In this respect, they are more similar to negative observations, used as vehicles to do complaints (Schegloff 1988a).

25. The "ok" with which this utterance begins is not a freestanding "ok" which could be understood as accepting SD's claim. As we will see, SD, himself, does not interpret this utterance as accepting his claim.

26. I thank John Heritage for access to the audiotape from this interview.

27. Given this discussion, it is now possible to see Debbie's turn in Excerpt 21, lines 21, 23–25 as a reversed polarity wh-question challenge, followed by an account for the assertion embedded in the challenge: "why wouldn:t- why wouldn't you go.=becu:z I mean (.) that's what Jay Tee told me you told hi:m,", i.e., "There's no other reason why you wouldn't go; I'm claiming this because that's what Jay Tee told me you told him." "Because" is used in this excerpt, as in Excerpts 10, 28 and 30, to introduce a warrant for a claim.

28. Those designed as "what do you mean" + partial repeat of a prior turn may be an exception. They do seem to convey a type of negative assertion. Marsha's challenge in Excerpt 35, for example, "Waddiyou mean you weren't harming anybuddy", does seem to convey something like "You can't possibly mean you weren't harming anybody."

29. I thank Ashley Scarborough for access to this data segment.

30. My thanks to Makoto Hayashi for pointing this out.

31. Jacoby (1998) notes that comment sessions after practice conference presentations done by a team of physicists are taken up predominantly with problematic aspects of the performance; it is in this way that members are socialized into the norms of effective physics conference presentations. Group members do not characterize these comment sessions as ego-damaging, but view them as necessary preparation for the actual conference talk. The writing conferences in this study were also made up predominantly of talk that addressed problems in the drafts; this talk seems to have a similar socializing function.

32. John Heritage, in a personal communication, suggests that there is a more general observation about authority and its interaction with preference structure to be made here, i.e., that giving a preferred response to a first pair part which is in some way against one's interest (e.g., a criticism of one's performance, or a command which would inconvenience someone) exemplifies the operation of authority. Giving a dispreferred response to such an utterance by someone in authority erodes that authority.

33. This data excerpt is taken from Schegloff (1995b, to appear).

34. Repeats to register receipt of a prior utterance are not usually done with upward intonation. Schegloff (personal communication) suggests that what this teacher may be doing is similar to "doing writing in an interactional context", e.g., when someone is writing something down that they are being told, and are saying the words as they are writing them down. Those repeats are done with upward intonation.

35. As discussed in the explication of Excerpt 36, Chapter 3, Rubin's "whaddyou mean" + repetition of the trouble source turn (lines 10–11) is taken to be expressing trouble understanding Kathy's turn in lines 5–6:

```
05   Kat:      It wove itself once it was set
06             up.=
07   Fre:      =Its woo:l?
08   Kat:      It's wool.
09             (0.8)
```

```
10  Rub:   -->  Whaddyou mean it wove itself once
11               it w's set up.=
12               =[What d's that] mean.=
13  Kat:         =[Oh i-        ]
14  Kat:         =Well I mean it's ve:ry simple,
```

These "what do you mean" repair initiations are not to be confused with "what do you mean" challenges, also discussed in Chapter 3.

36. These data were collected and transcribed by Jen Carder.

37. It might be objected that Eriko is a not fully proficient speaker of English and therefore is not using this type of repair in a native-like manner. However, the fact the both Jan and Geri do eventually hear Eriko's repairs as eliciting clarification rather than confirmation shows that this practice can be used to convey this action. It is interesting though that, in spite of Eriko's limited English proficiency, her repetitions are always at first taken to be candidate hearings proffered for confirmation. It may be that, with adults at least, even with those who have limited proficiency in a language, repair is generally at first taken to express problems with hearing rather than problems with competency.

38. The trouble source may or may not be said in the context of background noise, and this also enters into how the repair initiation is interpreted.

39. Excerpt 58 is taken directly from Quirk and Greenbaum (1973:198). Their use of a question mark at the end of the alternative question does not indicate rising intonation as it does in conversation analytic transcripts.

40. The first part of this excerpt, up to line 46, is discussed by Schegloff (1995b, to appear).

41. I thank Mi-Suk Seo for access to this data segment and the audiotape from which it was transcribed.

42. English for Specific Purposes classes are classes in English as a Second Language developed specifically for professionals in a particular field, such as for business students or medical professionals.

43. I would like to thank Hansun Zhang Waring for access to this data segment and to the audiotape from which it was transcribed.

44. Tamar is a native speaker of Hebrew, not English. This may be why she does not end the first alternative with upward intonation, as is usual with alternative questions.

45. And not all error correction is done as *repair*, i.e., interrupts the ongoing sequence of talk to deal with problems in speaking, hearing, or understanding the talk. Sometimes, rather than interrupting the ongoing sequence, speakers "embed" (Jefferson 1987) error correction in the next sequentially-appropriate turn of talk, as in the following example from Jefferson (1987:93):

```
01  Customer:    MM, the wales are wider apart
02               than that.
03  Salesman:    Okay, let me see if I can
04          -->  find one with wider threads
```

46. I thank Mi-Suk Seo for permission to use this data segment, which she collected and transcribed.

47. As explained by Schegloff (1997a), this practice is not a form of repair as defined by conversation analysts. In the example provided, the focal turn does not interrupt the ongoing talk to deal with trouble in hearing or understanding that talk. It is, instead, a response to Wesley's prior turn, a disagreement with it. This is a relevant next response to a "B-event" statement (Labov & Fanshel 1977), one that makes claims about a matter within the recipient's domain of knowledge. These types of claims are regularly responded to by confirmations or denials (Heritage & Roth 1995). The "me?" at the beginning of the turn is a common form for other-initiated repair, but here it is not responded to as a separate repair initiation, nor is Virginia inviting a response as if this were a repair; she immediately goes on to reject Wesley's claim.

48. Of course, learning also occurs through observation in North American cultures. Teachers introduce new material through lectures, and audiences observe master cooks during televised cooking classes. There does, however, seem to be a preference for learning through assisted performance; novices, including novice writers, novice swimmers, and novice speakers in a second language, are encouraged to attempt assisted performance before they are fully competent, in order to learn.

49. Adapted from Atkinson and Heritage (1984). There is some variation among transcripts from different sources.

References

Atkinson, J. M. & Heritage, J. (Eds.). (1984). *Structures of Social Action: Studies in Conversation Analysis*. Cambridge: Cambridge University Press.

Bolinger, D. L. M. (1957). *Interrogative Structures of American English: The Direct Question, Publication of the American Dialect Society, No. 28*. University, Alabama: University of Alabama Press.

Bruner, J. S. (1975). "The Ontogenesis of Speech Acts." *Journal of Child Language, 2*, 1–19.

Cazden, C. B. (1988). *Classroom Discourse: The Language of Teaching and Learning*. Portsmouth, NH: Heinemann.

Clayman, S. E. (2002). "'Unanswerable' Questions: *How* as an Interrogative Form." Paper presented at the American Sociological Association Annual Meeting, Chicago.

Clayman, S. E. & Heritage, J. (2002). "Questioning Presidents: Journalistic Deference and Adversarialness in the Press Conferences of U.S. Presidents Eisenhower and Reagan." *Journal of Communication, 2*, 749–775.

Clayman, S. E. (1988). "Displaying Neutrality in Television News Interviews." *Social Problems, 35*, 474–492.

Clayman, S. E. (1992). "Footing in the Achievement of Neutrality: The Case of News-Interview Discourse." In P. Drew & J. Heritage (Eds.), *Talk at Work: Interaction in Institutional Settings* (pp. 163–198). Cambridge: Cambridge University Press.

Clayman, S. E. & Gill, V. T. (2004). "Conversation Analysis." In A. Bryman & M. Hardy (Eds.), *Handbook of Data Analysis* (pp. 589–606). Beverly Hills: Sage.

Crago, M. B. (1992). "Communicative Interaction and Second Language Acquisition: An Inuit Example." *TESOL Quarterly, 26*(3), 487–505.

Drew, P. (1981). "Adults' Corrections of Children's Mistakes: A Response to Wells and Montgomery." In P. French & M. MacLure (Eds.), *Adult-Child Conversation: Studies in Structure and Process* (pp. 244–267). London: Croom Helm.

Drew, P. (1997). "'Open' Class Repair Initiators in Response to Sequential Sources of Troubles in Conversation." *Journal of Pragmatics, 28*, 69–101.

Drew, P. & Heritage, J. (1992a). "Analyzing Talk at Work: An Introduction." In P. Drew & J. Heritage (Eds.), *Talk at Work* (pp. 3–65). Cambridge: Cambridge University Press.

Drew, P. & Heritage, J. (1992b). *Talk at Work: Interaction in Institutional Settings*. Cambridge: Cambridge University Press.

Egbert, M. (1996). "Context-Sensitivity in Conversation: Eye Gaze and the German Repair Initiator Bitte?" *Language in Society, 25*(4), 587–612.

Egbert, M. (1997). "Some Interactional Achievements of Other-Initiated Repair in Multiperson Conversation." *Journal of Pragmatics, 27*, 611–634.

Fanselow, J. F. (1988). "'Let's See': Contrasting Conversations About Teaching." *TESOL Quarterly, 22*(1), 113–130.

Ford, C. E. (1993). *Grammar and Interaction: Adverbial Clauses in American English Conversations.* Cambridge, England: Cambridge University Press.

Freed, A. F. (1994). "The Form and Function of Questions in Informal Dyadic Conversation." *Journal of Pragmatics, 21,* 621–644.

Gardner, H. (1996). "Leading Minds: An Anatomy of Leadership." Reprinted in APS (Academic Publishing Service) Reader for ESL 35, ESL Service Courses, University of California, Los Angeles.

Goffman, E. (1981). *Forms of Talk.* Oxford: Blackwell.

Goodwin, C. (1986). "Gestures as a Resource for the Organization of Mutual Orientation." *Semiotica, 62*(1/2), 29–49.

Halliday, M. & Hasan, R. (1976). *Cohesion in English.* London: Longman.

Heath, S. B. (1983). *Ways with Words: Language, Life and Work in Communities and Classrooms.* Cambridge: Cambridge University Press.

Heritage, J. (1984a). "A Change-of-State Token and Aspects of Its Sequential Placement." In J. M. Atkinson & J. Heritage (Eds.), *Structures of Social Action: Studies in Conversation Analysis* (pp. 299–345). New York: Cambridge University Press.

Heritage, J. (1984b). *Garfinkel and Ethnomethodology.* Cambridge: Polity Press.

Heritage, J. (1985). "Analyzing News Interviews: Aspects of the Production of Talk for an Overhearing Audience." In T. A. v. Dijk (Ed.), *Handbook of Discourse Analysis* (pp. 95–119). London: Academic Press.

Heritage, J. (2002a). "Designing Questions and Setting Agendas in the News Interview." In P. Glenn, C. LeBaron, & J. Mandelbaum (Eds.), *Studies in Language and Social Interaction* (pp. 57–90). Mahwah, NJ: Erlbaum.

Heritage, J. (2002b). "The Limits of Questioning: Negative Interrogatives and Hostile Question Content." *Journal of Pragmatics, 34*(10–11), 1427–1446.

Heritage, J. & Greatbatch, D. L. (1991). "On the Institutional Character of Institutional Talk: The Case of News Interviews." In D. Boden & D. H. Zimmerman (Eds.), *Talk and Social Structure* (pp. 93–137). Berkeley: University of California Press.

Heritage, J. & Raymond, G. (2005). "The Terms of Agreement: Indexing Epistemic Authority and Subordination in Assessment Sequences." *Social Psychology Quarterly, 68*(1), 15–38.

Heritage, J. & Roth, A. L. (1995). "Grammar and Institution: Questions and Questioning in the Broadcast News Interview." *Research on Language and Social Interaction, 28*(1), 1–60.

Horn, L. R. (1978). "Some Aspects of Negation." In J. H. Greenberg, C. A. Ferguson, & E. A. Moravcsik (Eds.), *Universals of Human Language, Vol 4: Syntax* (pp. 127–210). Stanford: Stanford University Press.

Hosoda, Y. (2000). "Other-Repair in Japanese Conversations between Nonnative and Native Speakers." *Issues in Applied Linguistics, 11*(1), 39–63.

Hosoda, Y. (2001). "Conditions for Other-Repair in NS/NNS Conversation." *The Language Teacher, 25*(11), 29–31.

Jacoby, S. (1998). "Science as Performance: Socializing Scientific Discourse through the Conference Talk Rehearsal." Unpublished doctoral dissertation, University of California, Los Angeles.

Jacoby, S. & Gonzales, P. (2002). "Saying What Wasn't Said: Negative Observation as a Linguistic Resource for the Interactional Achievement of Performance Feedback." In C. E. Ford, B. A. Fox, & S. A. Thompson (Eds.) *The Language of Turn and Sequence.* Oxford: Oxford University Press.

Jefferson, G. (1974). "Error Correction as an Interactional Resource." *Language in Society, 2,* 181–199.

Jefferson, G. (1987). "On Exposed and Embedded Correction in Conversation." In G. Button & J. R. Lee (Eds.), *Talk and Social Organisation* (pp. 86–100). Clevedon: Multilingual Matters.

Kim, K.-H. (1999). "Other-Initiated Repair Sequences in Korean Conversation: Types and Functions." *Discourse and Cognition, 6*(2), 141–168.

Kim, K.-H. (2001). "Confirming Intersubjectivity through Retroactive Elaboration: Organization of Phrasal Units in Other-Initiated Repair Sequences in Korean Conversation." In M. Selting & E. Couper-Kuhlen (Eds.), *Studies in Interactional Linguistics.* Amsterdam: John Benjamins.

Koshik, I. (2002a). "A Conversation Analytic Study of Yes/No Questions Which Convey Reversed Polarity Assertions." *Journal of Pragmatics, 34*(12), 1851–1877.

Koshik, I. (2002b). "Designedly Incomplete Utterances: A Pedagogical Practice for Eliciting Knowledge Displays in Error Correction Sequences." *Research on Language and Social Interaction, 5*(3), 277–309.

Koshik, I. (2003). "Wh-Questions Used as Challenges." *Discourse Studies, 5*(1), 51–77.

Koshik, I. (2005). "Alternative Questions Used in Conversational Repair." *Discourse Studies, 7*(2), 193–211.

Labov, W. & Fanshel, D. (1977). *Therapeutic Discourse: Psychotherapy as Conversation.* New York: Academic Press.

Lerner, G. H. (1987). "Collaborative Turn Sequences: Sentence Construction and Social Action." Unpublished doctoral dissertation, University of California, Irvine.

Lerner, G. H. (1989). "Notes on Overlap Management in Conversation: The Case of Delayed Completion." *Western Journal of Speech Communication, 53,* 167–177.

Lerner, G. H. (1991). "On the Syntax of Sentences-in-Progress." *Language in Society, 20,* 441–458.

Lerner, G. H. (1996). "On the "Semi-Permeable" Character of Grammatical Units in Conversation: Conditional Entry into the Turn Space of Another Speaker." In E. Ochs, E. A. Schegloff, & S. A. Thompson (Eds.), *Interaction and Grammar* (pp. 238–276). Cambridge: Cambridge University Press.

Levinson, S. C. (1979). "Activity Types and Language." *Linguistics, 17,* 365–399.

Levinson, S. C. (1983). *Pragmatics.* New York: Cambridge University Press.

Maynard, D. (1984). *Inside Plea Bargaining: The Language of Negotiation.* New York: Plenum.

Mehan, H. (1979a). *Learning Lessons: Social Organization in the Classroom.* Cambridge, MA: Harvard University Press.

Mehan, H. (1979b). "'What Time Is It, Denise?': Asking Known Information Questions in Classroom Discourse." *Theory into Practice, 18*(4), 285–294.

Mehan, H. (1985). "The Structure of Classroom Discourse." In T. A. v. Dijk (Ed.), *Handbook of Discourse Analysis* (pp. 119–131). London: Academic Press.

Ochs, E. & Schieffelin, B. B. (1984). "Language Acquisition and Socialization: Three Developmental Stories and Their Implications." In R. A. Shweder & R. A. LeVine (Eds.), *Culture Theory: Essays on Mind, Self and Emotion* (pp. 276–320). New York: Cambridge University Press.

Pomerantz, A. (1978). "Compliment Responses: Notes on the Co-Operation of Multiple Constraints." In J. Schenkein (Ed.), *Studies in the Organization of Conversational Interaction* (pp. 79–112). New York: Academic Press.

Pomerantz, A. (1984). "Agreeing and Disagreeing with Assessments: Some Features of Preferred/Dispreferred Turn Shapes." In J. M. Atkinson & J. Heritage (Eds.), *Structures of Social Action* (pp. 57–101). Cambridge: Cambridge University Press.

Pomerantz, A. (1988). "Offering a Candidate Answer." *Communication Monographs, 55*(4), 360–373.

Poole, D. (1992). "Language Socialization in the Second Language Classroom." *Language Learning, 42*(4), 593–616.

Quirk, R. & Greenbaum, S. (1973). *A Concise Grammar of Contemporary English*. New York: Harcourt Brace Jovanovich.

Quirk, R., Greenbaum, S., Leech, G., & Svartvik, J. (1985). *A Comprehensive Grammar of the English Language*. New York: Longman.

Raymond, G. (2000). "The Structure of Responding: Type-Conforming and Nonconforming Responses to Yes/No Type Interrogatives." Unpublished doctoral dissertation, University of California, Los Angeles.

Sacks, H. (1987 [1973]). "On the Preferences for Agreement and Contiguity in Sequences in Conversation." In G. Button & J. R. Lee (Eds.), *Talk and Social Organisation* (pp. 54–69). Clevedon, England: Multilingual Matters.

Sacks, H. (1992). *Lectures on Conversation*. Edited by G. Jefferson. Vols. 1 & 2. Oxford: Blackwell.

Sacks, H., Schegloff, E. A., & Jefferson, G. (1974). "A Simplest Systematics for the Organization of Turn Taking for Conversation." *Language, 50*(4), 696–735.

Schegloff, E. A. (1968). "Sequencing in Conversational Openings." *American Anthropologist, 70*, 1075–1095.

Schegloff, E. A. (1972). "Notes on a Conversational Practice: Formulating Place." In D. Sudnow (Ed.), *Studies in Social Interaction* (pp. 75–119). New York: Free Press.

Schegloff, E. A. (1979). "The Relevance of Repair to Syntax-for-Conversation." In T. Givon (Ed.), *Syntax and Semantics 12: Discourse and Syntax* (pp. 261–286). New York: Academic Press.

Schegloff, E. A. (1981). "Discourse as an Interactional Achievement: Some Uses of 'Uh Huh' and Other Things That Come between Sentences." In D. Tannen (Ed.), *Analyzing Discourse: Text and Talk* (pp. 71–93). Washington, DC: Georgetown University Press.

Schegloff, E. A. (1984). "On Some Questions and Ambiguities in Conversation." In J. M. Atkinson & J. Heritage (Eds.), *Structures of Social Action* (pp. 28–52). Cambridge: Cambridge University Press.

Schegloff, E. A. (1987a). "Analyzing Single Episodes of Interaction: An Exercise in Conversation Analysis." *Social Psychology Quarterly, 50*(2), 101–114.

Schegloff, E. A. (1987b). "Some Sources of Misunderstanding in Talk-in-Interaction." *Linguistics, 25*(1), 201–218.

Schegloff, E. A. (1988a). "Goffman and the Analysis of Conversation." In P. Drew & A. Wooton (Eds.), *Erving Goffman: Exploring the Interaction Order* (pp. 89–135). Oxford: Polity Press.

Schegloff, E. A. (1988b). "On an Actual Virtual Servo-Mechanism for Guessing Bad News: A Single Case Conjecture." *Social Problems, 35*(4), 442–457.

Schegloff, E. A. (1992). "Repair after Next Turn: The Last Structurally Provided Defense of Intersubjectivity in Conversation." *American Journal of Sociology, 97*(5), 1295–1345.

Schegloff, E. A. (1995a). "Discourse as an Interactional Achievement III: The Omnirelevance of Action." *Research on Language and Social Interaction, 28*(3), 185–211.

Schegloff, E. A. (1995b). "Sequence Organization." Unpublished manuscript.

Schegloff, E. A. (1997a). "Practices and Actions: Boundary Cases of Other-Initiated Repair." *Discourse Processes, 23*, 499–545.

Schegloff, E. A. (1997b). "Third Turn Repair." In G. Guy, C. Feagin, D. Schiffrin, & J. Baugh (Eds.), *Towards a Social Science of Language: Papers in Honor of William Labov. Volume 2: Social Interaction and Discourse Structures* (pp. 31–40). Philadelphia: John Benjamins.

Schegloff, E. A. (2000). "When 'Others' Initiate Repair." *Applied Linguistics, 21*(2), 205–243.

Schegloff, E. A. (to appear). *A Primer of Conversation Analysis: Sequence Organization.* Cambridge: Cambridge University Press.

Schegloff, E. A., Jefferson, G., & Sacks, H. (1977). "The Preference for Self-Correction in the Organization of Repair in Conversation." *Language, 53*(2), 361–382.

Schegloff, E. A., Koshik, I., Jacoby, S., & Olsher, D. (2002). "Conversation Analysis and Applied Linguistics." *Annual Review of Applied Linguistics, 22*, Discourse and Dialog, 3–31.

Schegloff, E. A. & Sacks, H. (1973). "Opening up Closings." *Semiotica, 8*, 289–327.

Schieffelin, B. B. (1990). *The Give and Take of Everyday Life: Language Socialization of Kaluli Children.* New York: Cambridge University Press.

Scollon, R. & Scollon, S. B. K. (1981). *Narrative, Literacy and Face in Interethnic Communication.* Norwood, NJ: Ablex.

Searle, J. R. (1969). *Speech Acts: An Essay in the Philosophy of Language.* Cambridge: Cambridge University Press.

Sinclair, J. M. & Coulthard, R. M. (1975). *Towards an Analysis of Discourse: The English Used by Teachers and Pupils.* London: Oxford University Press.

Taylor, C. E. (1995). "'You Think It Was a Fight?': Co-Constructing (the Struggle for) Meaning, Face, and Family in Everyday Narrative Activity." *Research on Language and Social Interaction, 28*(3), 283–317.

ten Have, P. (1999). *Doing Conversation Analysis: A Practical Guide.* London: Sage.

Weber, E. G. (1993). *Varieties of Questions in English Conversation.* Edited by S. A. Thompson & P. J. Hopper. Vol. 3, *Studies in Discourse and Grammar.* Amsterdam: John Benjamins.

Wong, J. (2000). "Delayed Next Turn Repair Initiation in Native/Nonnative Speaker English Conversation." *Applied Linguistics, 21*, 274–297.

Yoon, K.-E. (in progress). "Complaint Talk in Korean Conversation." Unpublished doctoral dissertation, University of Illinois at Urbana-Champaign.

Zaleznik, A. (1984). "Charismatic and Consensus Leaders: A Psychological Comparison." In W. E. Rosenback & R. L. Taylor (Eds.), *Contemporary Issues in Leadership* (pp. 255–270). Boulder, CO: Westview Press.

Zimmerman, D. H. (1988). "On Conversation: The Conversation Analytic Perspective." In J. Anderson (Ed.), *Communication Yearbook 11* (pp. 406–432). Beverly Hills, CA: Sage.

Name index

A
Atkinson, J. Maxwell   163, 167

B
Bolinger, Dwight L. M.   2, 11, 12, 40, 70, 124, 163
Bruner, Jerome S.   155

C
Cazden, Courtney B.   155
Clayman, Steven E.   3, 25, 26, 49–51, 61, 150, 163
Coulthard, R. Malcolm   155
Crago, Martha B.   154, 155

D
Drew, Paul   27, 55, 59, 71, 112, 145, 148, 155, 163

E
Egbert, Maria   112

F
Fanselow, John F.   156
Fanshel, David   1, 167
Ford, Cecilia E.   25, 147
Freed, Alice F.   2

G
Gill, Virginia T.   163
Goffman, Erving   92
Gonzales, Patrick   81, 153
Goodwin, Charles   92

Greatbatch, David   61, 150
Greenbaum, Sidney   116, 166

H
Halliday, Michael   46
Hasan, Ruqaiya   46
Heath, Shirley B.   155
Heritage, John   1, 3, 5, 10, 12, 15–17, 25, 26, 55, 59–61, 71, 86, 103, 116, 123, 141, 143, 145, 148, 150, 163, 165, 167
Horn, Laurence R.   27, 40
Hosoda, Yuri   112

J
Jacoby, Sally   81, 153, 156, 165
Jefferson, Gail   104, 112, 166

K
Kim, Kyu-hyun   112
Koshik, Irene   107, 112, 116, 164

L
Labov, William   1, 167
Lerner, Gene   58, 164
Levinson, Stephen C.   71, 148, 163

M
Maynard, Douglas   55
Mehan, Hugh   34, 76, 109, 129, 149, 155

O
Ochs, Elinor   154, 163

P
Pomerantz, Anita   10, 20, 31, 163
Poole, Deborah   154

Q
Quirk, Randolf   1, 2, 10, 11, 21, 22, 33, 40, 116, 152, 164, 166

R
Raymond, Geoffrey   10, 116
Roth, Andrew L.   1, 167

S
Sacks, Harvey   4, 10, 13, 31, 32, 43, 56, 84, 98, 104
Schegloff, Emanuel A.   1–4, 9, 10, 13–16, 21, 27–29, 31, 33, 34, 43, 52, 56, 61, 63, 64, 66, 75, 81, 94, 95, 98, 99, 102, 104, 108, 112, 113, 115, 127, 128, 141, 145, 152, 153, 156, 159, 163–167
Schieffelin, Bambi B.   24, 152, 154, 156
Scollon, Ron   154, 155
Scollon, Suzanne B. K.   154, 155
Searle, John R.   34, 149
Sinclair, John   155

T
Taylor, Carolyn E.   22, 23
ten Have, Paul   4

W
Weber, Elizabeth G.   1, 21, 22, 33, 152
Wong, Jean   112

Y
Yoon, Kyung-eun   3, 53, 54, 164

Z
Zimmerman, Donald H.   163

Subject index

A

academic
 ~ audience   32, 59, 84, 164
 ~ discourse norms   32, 59, 71, 84, 153, 158
  see also norms
account   20, 22, 25, 42, 43, 45, 47–49, 51, 52, 54, 57, 58, 60, 61, 65, 69, 84, 90, 126, 131, 141, 147, 165
 see also grounds
accountable   31, 57, 60, 90, 93
accusation   17, 18, 20–22, 24, 36, 37, 40–49, 51, 54, 57, 59, 61, 70, 149
action
 course of ~   10, 16, 36, 43, 72, 98, 100, 101, 103, 107, 108, 112, 132, 144, 150
 trajectory of ~   10, 97, 98
 see also sequence
adjacency   43, 46, 64, 66
 ~ pair   9
adjacent positioning   43, 45, 46, 64, 66, 147
adversarialness   61, 150
alignment   9, 10, 13, 15, 16, 21, 24, 26, 27, 31, 32, 34, 36, 37, 49, 50, 53, 56, 65, 69, 72, 73, 77, 78, 82, 84, 87, 91 94–96, 99, 128, 147, 155, 157, 158, 163, 164
 see also disalign
 see also preference: preferred response
alternate hearings   58, 111, 117, 119, 121, 123, 125, 142, 144, 145, 157
 see also clarification of ~
 see also repair

alternative question   111, 116–145, 148–150, 153–155, 157, 166
anaphora   43, 46, 76, 80, 90, 93, 147
animate   92
argument   20, 21, 39, 66, 67, 119
assertion   *see* reversed polarity assertion
audience   *see* academic audience
authority   24, 165
 see also epistemic authority

B

B-event   1
backdown   9, 14, 16, 28, 34, 47, 56, 57, 126, 131, 136, 148, 152
background   29, 31–34, 56–59, 84, 85
because clause   25, 58, 60, 61, 65, 147–148, 165
broadcast news
 see also press conference
 ~ interview   1, 3, 12, 13, 15–20, 24–27, 36, 54, 55, 59–61, 148–151
 ~ interviewee   12, 15, 17, 18, 27, 36, 59–61, 150, 151
 ~ interviewer   3, 12, 13, 15–18, 24, 26, 27, 36, 59–61, 149, 150

C

candidate
 ~ answer   20
 ~ correction   *see* correction: candidate correction
 ~ hearing   29, 33, 35, 113, 115, 117, 123, 124, 126, 131, 135–137, 142, 145, 166
  see also repair

change of state token   103
   see also oh
claim   2, 16, 24, 27, 34, 36, 44, 46, 47, 54,
      57–60, 64, 65, 70, 116, 131, 143,
      147, 149, 151–153, 157, 165, 167
   ~ understanding   157
   ~ to knowledge   24, 27, 34, 36, 70,
      116, 143, 149, 153
      see also epistemic position
      see also epistemic stance
      see also epistemic strength
      see also knowledge
clarification   22, 66, 78, 81, 108,
      117–123, 139, 142–145, 153, 166
   see also repair
   ~ of alternate hearings,   111,
      117–121, 142–144
      see also alternate hearings
   ~ of alternate understandings   111,
      121–123, 142–144
   request for ~   66, 166
collaborative completion   58, 59, 115
complaint   1, 3, 40, 47, 49, 51–54, 62–64,
      70, 81, 119, 122, 164
compliment   66, 119, 121
conditional relevance   4
conduciveness   9–13, 36, 40, 124
conference   see press conference, see
      writing conference
confirmation of a hearing   29, 103
   see also repair
congruent preferences   see preference:
      congruent preferences
continuer   75
contrastive stress   see stress: contrastive
      stress
conversation analysis   3–5
correction   28–36, 61, 69, 99–109, 111,
      113, 115, 116, 123–145,
      147–150, 152–157, 166
   see also error
   see also repair
   candidate ~   111, 124–145, 148,
      153, 154, 157

eliciting ~   34–37, 59, 103, 104,
      111, 123, 126, 129, 132, 133,
      143–145, 147, 148, 157
   other-correction   69, 115, 126, 127,
      152, 156
   prompt for self-correction   29, 69,
      101, 103–105, 107, 111, 115, 137
   self-correction   28–37, 59, 99–109,
      115, 116, 123, 126, 137, 143,
      145, 149, 153
criticism   23, 32, 56, 70, 72, 73, 76,
      80–82, 84, 88, 90, 92–94,
      98–101, 107, 119, 128, 129, 131,
      137, 140, 147–149, 154–156, 165
   mitigate ~   155–157

D

declarative question   1, 21, 22, 33, 152,
      154
deixis   66, 92, 118, 119, 131, 137, 154
   deictic pronoun   137
   deictic reference   66, 92, 119, 131
denial   17, 21–23, 42, 43, 45, 47, 48, 151,
      152, 167
design, turn and sequence   3, 10, 11, 13,
      16, 24, 36, 39, 43, 44, 54, 56, 57,
      59–61, 64, 66, 67, 71, 86, 92–97,
      114, 117, 125, 126, 134, 135,
      137, 143, 144, 147–149, 155, 158
   see also recipient design
designedly incomplete utterance   107
direct quote   26
disagreement   5, 10, 13–18, 22, 27–29,
      33, 34, 36, 37, 40, 56, 57, 59, 60,
      64, 65, 67, 69, 70, 81, 95, 126,
      127, 131, 148, 152, 167
   see also pre-disagreement
   see also preference: dispreferred
      response
disalign   37, 147
   see also alignment
   see also preference: dispreferred
      response
display question   see known information
      question

dispreferred
  ~ manner *see* preference: dispreferred manner
  ~ response *see* preference: dispreferred response
downgrade 15, 16, 156

E
epistemic
  see also claim to knowledge
  ~ authority 13–16, 27, 34, 116, 135, 143, 145, 149, 153, 154
  ~ environment 16, 163
  ~ position 16, 17, 27, 28
  ~ qualifier 81
  ~ stance 12–16, 21, 36, 39, 40, 47, 49, 54, 60, 63, 64, 84, 90, 94, 97, 111, 123, 126, 128, 139, 144, 163, 164
  ~ strength 14, 15, 24, 27, 34, 36, 40, 69, 149, 156
error 29, 35, 67, 69, 99–109, 115–116, 121–145, 147, 152, 153
  ~ correction *see* correction
  see also repair
  grammar ~ 67, 69, 99–109
  lexical ~ 35, 116, 121–123
evaluation 29, 34, 36, 37, 77, 80–82, 104, 107, 138–140, 149, 153, 155–157
  ~ position 34–37, 149
expert 31, 34, 59, 70, 94, 154, 155, 164

F
footing 25, 26
framing 92

G
gesture 3, 92
goals *see* institutional goals
grounds 54, 57, 59, 61, 63–65, 151, 152
  see also account

H
hint 72, 77, 99–109, 134, 142, 147–149, 155, 157

I
increment 58, 134, 135, 137–141, 144, 163
  increment-like addition 58, 60, 64, 147, 148
inferential framework 71, 148
informing 154, 156
  response to ~ 103
institutional
  ~ context 61
  ~ goals 31, 55, 59, 61, 71, 72, 111, 148, 157
  ~ norms 55, 61, 71, 148, 150
    see also norms
  ~ setting 54, 55, 59, 71, 148, 150, 163
institutionally specific practices 71, 148
interrogative 1
interview *see* broadcast news interview
interviewee *see* broadcast news interviewee
interviewer *see* broadcast news interviewer
intonation 1, 28, 33–36, 56, 69, 81, 93, 102–104, 112, 115–117, 123, 131, 134, 135, 137, 139, 149, 153, 154, 161, 165, 166
  see also prosody
invitation 1, 4, 49, 95, 114, 115
  see also pre-invitation

J
joke 51, 121, 127–128
justification 31, 33, 42, 56, 60, 61, 86, 87, 90, 93, 98, 164
  request for ~ 31, 90, 93, 98

K
knowledge
  see also claim to knowledge
  access to ~ 11
  ~ base 16, 29, 35, 70
  ~ display 72, 101
  ~ domain 24, 35, 36, 40, 70, 149
  ~ state 16, 36, 72, 97, 103, 149

known information question   34, 35, 76, 91, 96, 106, 109, 129, 149, 155
Korean   3, 53, 54, 136, 164

L
language acquisiton   123
   see also socialization
laughter   32, 35, 36, 90, 128
learner   111, 123, 124, 129, 144, 145, 147, 148, 153, 156
   see also novice
learning   82, 94, 141, 154, 155, 167

M
multiple preferences   see preference: multiple preferences

N
negative
   ~ event   81
   ~ observation   76, 81, 153, 156, 164
   ~ polarity   see polarity: negative polarity
neutralistic stance   61, 150
neutrality   26, 150
news interview   see broadcast news interview
non-present parties   24–27, 36, 49–51, 147
norms   24, 32, 55, 59, 61, 71, 84, 148, 150, 152, 158, 165
   see also academic discourse norms
   see also institutional norms
noticing   81, 103, 156
novice   31, 59, 154, 155, 167
   see also learner

O
oh   103, 123, 141, 143
   see also change of state token
okay   141
opinion   17, 37, 61, 152

P
parent/child interaction   22–24, 136–137

pedagogical talk   29–37, 55–59, 70–109, 111, 129–142, 144, 145, 147–150, 153–159, 163
   see also writing conference
   see also tutoring
phonological reduction   118
phonologically similar   117, 121, 125, 143
pitch   93, 117, 161
   see also prosody
polarity   2, 10, 11, 13, 15–17, 22, 27, 33, 36, 40, 69, 70, 93, 97, 149, 150, 164
   negative ~   27, 40, 97, 149, 164
   positive ~   11
   see also reversed polarity assertion
   see also reversed polarity question
practice   3–5
pre-disagreement   9, 14, 15, 27–37, 56, 57, 59, 115, 116, 136, 147, 152
   see also disagreement
pre-invitation   95
   see also invitation
preference   9–11, 13, 15, 16, 36, 72, 82, 94–96, 99–101, 108, 124, 144, 145, 148, 153–156, 158, 164, 165
   congruent preferences   94, 99, 108
   cross-cutting preferences   10, 108
   dispreferred action   28, 34, 152, 156
   dispreferred response   10, 15, 31, 36, 77, 86, 95–97, 99, 125, 142, 144, 148, 157, 163–165
      see also disalign
      see also disagreement
   dispreferred manner   65, 81, 86, 95, 131
   multiple preferences   94, 99, 100, 108
   ~ structure   9, 82, 94, 95, 99–101, 108, 144, 155, 156, 158, 165
   preferred manner   15, 34, 57, 77, 90, 91, 95
   preferred actions   156
   preferred response   10, 28, 33, 72, 77, 90, 91, 94–96, 99, 100,

Subject index **181**

108, 127, 132, 139, 144, 148, 155, 157, 158, 164, 165
   see also alignment
press conference   12, 13, 17, 59–61
   see also broadcast news interview
problem-solving   76, 98
proficiency, language   114, 166
prosody   10, 35, 133
   see also intonation
   see also pitch
   see also stress

Q

question   *see* alternative ~, *see* declarative ~, *see* known information ~, *see* rhetorical ~, *see* reversed polarity ~, *see* tag ~

R

really   11, 26, 27, 36, 86, 141, 149
recipient design   32, 56, 84, 164
register receipt   102, 165
relevant omission   81
repair   14–16, 27–37, 44, 56, 62, 63, 66, 67, 69, 104, 112–132, 136, 137, 142–144, 149, 158, 159, 163, 164, 166, 167
   see also alternate hearings
   see also candidate hearing
   see also clarification of alternate hearings
   see also clarification of alternate understandings
   see also clarification, request for
   see also confirmation of a hearing
   see also correction
   see also error
   see also trouble hearing
   see also trouble source
   see also trouble understanding
   other-completed ~   126
   other-initiated ~   27–37, 56, 66, 67, 104, 112–131, 144, 149, 167

~ initiation   16, 27–37, 56, 66, 67, 69, 112–131, 137, 143, 158, 159, 163, 166, 167
~ initiator   14, 15, 66, 67, 121, 124, 135
self-initiated ~   44, 62, 112
third position ~   62, 63
repetition   28, 29, 33–35, 56, 57, 66, 67, 69, 102, 104, 112, 114–116, 118, 119, 121, 123, 125–127, 131–134, 137, 142, 149, 152–154, 157, 165, 166
reported
   ~ actions   49, 51
   ~ speech   24–27, 36, 93, 147
reversed polarity
   ~ assertion   1, 2, 11–13, 15, 16, 27, 32, 33, 36, 39, 40, 43, 44, 47, 52, 54, 57–64, 69, 70, 72, 76–78, 81, 84, 90, 93–101, 103, 107, 108, 141, 147–152, 156, 164, 165
   ~ question   2, 13, 16, 36, 37, 111, 147, 150, 165
rhetorical question   2, 11, 24, 37, 40, 147, 156
role   6, 55, 59–61, 70, 71, 148, 154, 155
rush through   43, 45, 47

S

sanction   24, 36, 69, 152
scaffolding   155
second language   35, 55, 71, 121, 122, 129, 154, 156, 158, 166, 167
sequence   3, 4, 9, 10, 16, 24, 27, 33, 36, 40, 43, 70, 72, 76, 80–82, 92–95, 97–101, 104, 106–109, 111, 112, 126, 128, 135, 139, 144, 148–150, 152, 159, 166
sequential context   67, 71, 72, 98, 107, 135, 148, 149, 159
sequential implicativeness   61
sequential position   24, 36, 40, 43, 139, 149
sequentially appropriate response   40, 43, 70
   see also action

shaming   24, 152, 156
socialization   22, 24, 71, 94, 154, 165
　　see also language acquisition
solution   32, 33, 72, 76–78, 84, 90, 98,
　　99, 101, 103, 107–109, 148, 153
stance   12–16, 21, 36, 39–41, 47, 49, 50,
　　54, 60, 61, 63, 64, 84, 90, 94, 97,
　　111, 123, 126, 128, 139, 141,
　　144, 150, 163, 164
　　see also epistemic stance
state of knowledge   see knowledge state
stress   21, 23, 24, 26, 31, 35, 36, 52–54,
　　90, 103, 107, 115–117, 119, 126,
　　131, 133, 135, 137, 149
　　see also prosody
　　contrastive stress   23, 24, 26, 31, 36,
　　　52, 53, 90, 103, 115, 119, 126,
　　　131, 135, 137, 149
substitution   46, 64, 66, 147

T
tag question   15
teacher-student talk   see pedagogical talk

test question   see known information
　　question
thesis statement   74, 77, 78, 157
trouble
　　see also repair
　　∼ hearing   14, 121
　　∼ source   28, 67, 112–117, 121, 123,
　　　125–127, 131, 132, 134–137,
　　　141, 144, 148, 153, 154, 165, 166
　　∼ understanding   14, 114, 115, 165
tutoring   121–123
　　see also pedagogical talk
　　see also writing conference

U
unfair treatment   51–53

W
"why that now"   4, 43, 98
writing conference   29–34, 55–59,
　　70–109, 129–132, 134–142, 144,
　　148, 149, 153, 155
　　see also pedagogical talk
　　see also tutoring

In the series *Studies in Discourse and Grammar* the following titles have been published thus far or are scheduled for publication:

1. **GELUYKENS, Ronald:** From Discourse Process to Grammatical Construction. On Left-Dislocation in English. 1992. xii, 182 pp.
2. **IWASAKI, Shoichi:** Subjectivity in Grammar and Discourse. Theoretical considerations and a case study of Japanese spoken discourse. 1992. xii, 152 pp.
3. **WEBER, Elizabeth G.:** Varieties of Questions in English Conversation. 1993. x, 252 pp.
4. **DOWNING, Pamela A.:** Numeral Classifier Systems: The Case of Japanese. 1996. xx, 336 pp.
5. **TAO, Hongyin:** Units in Mandarin Conversation. Prosody, discourse, and grammar. 1996. xvi, 226 pp.
6. **DORGELOH, Heidrun:** Inversion in Modern English. Form and function. 1997. x, 236 pp.
7. **LAURY, Ritva:** Demonstratives in Interaction. The emergence of a definite article in Finnish. 1997. viii, 294 pp.
8. **MORI, Junko:** Negotiating Agreement and Disagreement in Japanese. Connective expressions and turn construction. 1999. xii, 240 pp.
9. **HELASVUO, Marja-Liisa:** Syntax in the Making. The emergence of syntactic units in Finnish conversation. 2001. xiv, 176 pp.
10. **SELTING, Margret and Elizabeth COUPER-KUHLEN (eds.):** Studies in Interactional Linguistics. 2001. viii, 438 pp.
11. **SCHEIBMAN, Joanne:** Point of View and Grammar. Structural patterns of subjectivity in American English conversation. 2002. xiv, 188 pp.
12. **HAYASHI, Makoto:** Joint Utterance Construction in Japanese Conversation. 2003. xii, 250 pp.
13. **ENGLEBRETSON, Robert:** Searching for Structure. The problem of complementation in colloquial Indonesian conversation. 2003. x, 206 pp.
14. **DU BOIS, John W., Lorraine E. KUMPF and William J. ASHBY (eds.):** Preferred Argument Structure. Grammar as architecture for function. 2003. x, 459 pp.
15. **GOLATO, Andrea:** Compliments and Compliment Responses. Grammatical structure and sequential organization. 2005. xii, 249 pp.
16. **KOSHIK, Irene:** Beyond Rhetorical Questions. Assertive questions in everyday interaction. 2005. x, 182 pp.
17. **HAKULINEN, Auli and Margret SELTING (eds.):** Syntax and Lexis in Conversation. Studies on the use of linguistic resources in talk-in-interaction. viii, 405 pp. + index. *Expected September 2005*